Enjoy
Your Journey!

Phyllis Karen

JOURNEYS
Tripping Through Life

Phyllis Karsnia

iUniverse LLC
Bloomington

JOURNEYS
TRIPPING THROUGH LIFE

Copyright © 2014 Phyllis Karsnia.

All rights reserved. No part of this book may be used or reproduced by any means, graphic, electronic, or mechanical, including photocopying, recording, taping or by any information storage retrieval system without the written permission of the publisher except in the case of brief quotations embodied in critical articles and reviews.

iUniverse books may be ordered through booksellers or by contacting:

iUniverse LLC
1663 Liberty Drive
Bloomington, IN 47403
www.iuniverse.com
1-800-Authors (1-800-288-4677)

Because of the dynamic nature of the Internet, any web addresses or links contained in this book may have changed since publication and may no longer be valid. The views expressed in this work are solely those of the author and do not necessarily reflect the views of the publisher, and the publisher hereby disclaims any responsibility for them.

Any people depicted in stock imagery provided by Thinkstock are models, and such images are being used for illustrative purposes only.
Certain stock imagery © Thinkstock.

ISBN: 978-1-4917-2999-1 (sc)
ISBN: 978-1-4917-3001-0 (hc)
ISBN: 978-1-4917-3000-3 (e)

Library of Congress Control Number: 2014906007

Printed in the United States of America.

iUniverse rev. date: 05/15/2014

Dedicated to my family:

My husband Leo: for encouraging me to travel and to write.

Allen: for forcing us to travel to new places to visit our grandchildren—Erin, Jacqueline, Kelly, and Bailey—as he moved from Minneapolis to Chicago to Boston to Houston.

Sherry: for living in International Falls so we had almost daily contact with our grandchildren, Adam and Jenna. And now, her grandchildren, Jenna and Luke's three children, Nissa Marie, Whitney Jean, and Cale Edward. Also, for being here when we need her and for her gourmet meals.

Jayne: for taking me traveling on many fun trips and sharing her son, Tyler, with us.

Thank you to:

My friends who encouraged me to write.
My fellow travelers who made these trips so enjoyable.
My brother and consultant, Donald St. Pierre.
Readers Susan Congrave, Mary Dahlen, Peggy Roeder,
and Nancy Kalstad for offering excellent suggestions.
To Sarah Griffith for creating the excellent maps for the book.

In memory of:

Marie Donahue Karsnia
Who started me on a book-writing journey

Contents

Introduction 1

1. The First 500 Miles 5
2. Caribbean Adventures 7
3. The Ironing Board—*Five Generations* 11
4. Canning Conversations 13
5. Tricky Squash 15
6. Portuguese Surprises 18
7. Roman Grandeur 22
8. Viennese Splendor 26
9. November Phenomenon 30
10. Flying Free, Jayne and Me 32
11. Superlative Shopping Excursion 39
12. Cruising the Aegean Sea 45
13. April in Paris 49
14. The Birch Tree 55
15. Loppet 57
16. Patterns on the Mountain 59
17. Ageless Magic 61
18. Searching Dublin for a Cousin 65
19. London's Hop on, Hop Off 69
20. Ireland's Terrible Trouble 72
21. Excitement at Gate 38 75
22. Serching for Skeletons 77
23. Irish Wonders 79
24. Newgrange Mystery 88
25. Scandinavian Tour—*Following the Flowers* 91
26. Syttende Mai 102
27. Asian Adventure 110
28. Fearful Feng Shui 115
29. Experiencing the Facilities 118
30. Maax and Me 121
31. Bailey Goes to Texas 123

32. Quebec Quest 126
33. NYC Theater Blast 135
34. A Working Mother's Journey 141
35. Sisters' Journeys 145
36. Earthy Spirituality 154

Introduction

Some authors compile stories from other authors; I've compiled stories from my own travel journals, with a few domestic adventures added for humor.

I'd already turned forty when I started traveling, I was too busy taking care of my family and working. I was thrilled to be a working woman—thrilled with my battered wood desk and manual typewriter when I was hired as an insurance clerk at Minnesota and Ontario Paper Company in 1963. After working seven years as a part-time LPN at Falls Memorial Hospital, usually on the 3:30 to 11:00 p.m. shift, I applied for the M&O job when I heard they were adding an insurance department to pay employees' medical claims on-site. My son, Allen, and daughter, Sherry, were both in school, a daytime job would give me more time with them. My mother volunteered to babysit my new baby, Jayne. I joked that I was the only nurse in town who could type and take shorthand, two skills required for the job along with medical terminology.

My friend, Marcelle, coaxed me away from my job at Boise Paper (formerly M&O) to take an authentic vacation to the Caribbean. The travel bug bit me! After that, I started traveling with Rainy River Travel Club and as much as I enjoyed the trips, I enjoyed journaling about them afterward as well. Wherever I went, my friends waited for the travel story.

Truly, I didn't realize how much I'd traveled until I gathered my stories. In addition, we once owned a trailer in Venture Out, a trailer park in Mesa, Arizona. We vacationed there two to three weeks each winter. While Allen and his family lived in Boston, we explored Massachusetts, Connecticut, Vermont, and Maine. Allen moved to Houston, and we now enjoy a few weeks in Texas.

Retiring from the human resources department at Boise Paper gave me the opportunity to take writing classes. Writing became a passion. As the Millennium approached, I had an *Aha* moment—my mother-in-law, Marie Karsnia, had lived most of the twentieth century, a living history lesson. The short stories I wrote from her anecdotes turned into a book, *A Bit of Irish Gold*

While revising *A Bit of Irish Gold* an idea percolated. Why couldn't I write a book based on my travels? Dragging out journals and photo albums to retrace my journeys, I remembered that on each trip I felt like I was living a dream. Is this really me exploring wonders of the world that I'd studied in school or read about or fantasized about? We're quite isolated in northern Minnesota; I appreciated seeing more of the world. I enjoyed reliving my travel journeys—I hope you enjoy them too.

A Gertrude Stein quote inspired me to add a few ordinary life events: "Anything one does every day is important and imposing and anywhere one lives is interesting and beautiful." I think all women are on a "journey of life" and we benefit from sharing our stories. Feel free to "trip" over facts and history you don't find interesting and laugh at my "tripping" episodes in domestic adventures.

Map of Minnesota

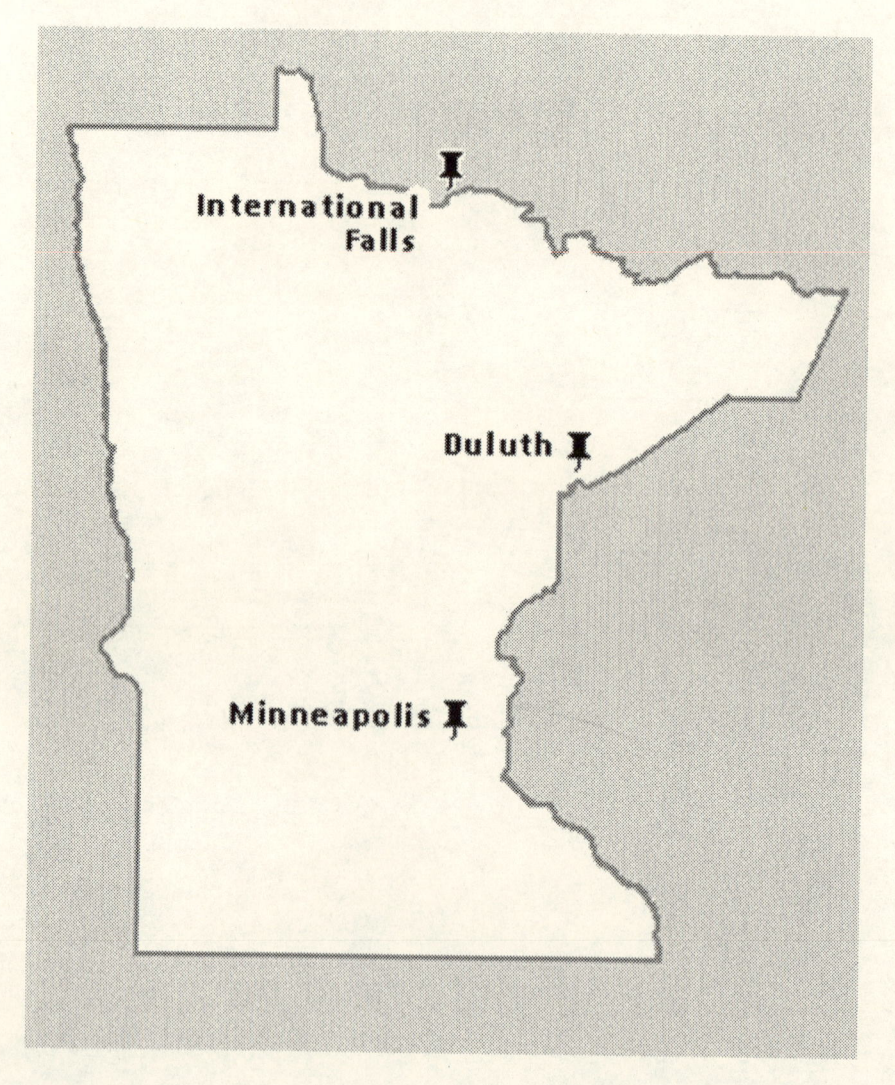

Chapter 1
The First 500 Miles
1950s— present

Highway 53 begins in International Falls, Minnesota and ends in LaCrosse, Wisconsin. That's how it seemed when I was a kid. At Mama's insistence, at least once a year we packed up Daddy's newest automobile and set off on the five hundred mile journey to visit my maternal grandparents and Mama's sisters who lived on the end of that road.

As an only child for thirteen years until my baby brother, Donnie, surprised us, I sat alone in the back seat reading a book or watching the scenery. Changing landscapes along the way absorbed me; I was thrilled to win an essay about Minnesota because of those trips. I wrote about our northern forests, southern Minnesota's rolling farmscapes, the beautiful bluffs surrounding the Mississippi River. Those trips made me love my state, but I really wanted to go to Disneyland like my friend, Tammy.

Grandma Ida, Aunt Edna, and Aunt Bernice ran rooming houses, three-storied, gray-shingled buildings tightly packed in a neighborhood with other ugly 1940s buildings. Yards were mere strips of grass with no place to play.

One summer day, bored from listening to my aunts' endless talk, talk, talking, I walked up and down in front of Grandma's, afraid of getting lost if I turned the corner. It was almost too hot to breathe on the concrete sidewalk; forlornly, I climbed into Daddy's car. I hated Mama's smoking, but defiantly I grabbed the pack of Lucky Strikes on the dashboard, pulled out a cigarette, and stuck it in my mouth. Lighting the match took several tries, and by the time I got the cigarette lit, I felt dizzy and nauseous. Sliding out of the car, stomping out the cigarette, I slammed the door on my thumb. Waving my bloody thumb, I ran howling into the house. My first and last cigarette.

On one trip, Mama let me stay in Stoddard, a suburb of LaCrosse, with Aunt Winnie and my favorite cousin, Marilyn. Following days filled with fun, it was comforting to be awakened in the still nights by the whooo-whooo from distant trains. I fantasized about riding on that speeding train as it whizzed by until I fell back to sleep.

Reading encouraged fantasizing, too, taking me away to interesting places. Snuggled in a comfy chair, savoring a Hersey bar one square at a time, I read until Mama interrupted my daydreaming journeys to peel potatoes or do other chores. I fell in love with *Heidi's* mountains in Switzerland, and when I wasn't having small town adventures with my best friend Maxine, I enjoyed escapades with *Betsy, Tacy, and Tib*. The five of us grew up together. Betsy wanted to be a writer; that might have planted a tiny seed, but in the 1950s there were only three options: secretary, nurse, or teacher. I prepared for all three in high school before choosing nursing.

As a student at St. Olaf College in Northfield, enrolled in a four-year nursing program, hitchhiking the forty miles to Minneapolis was daring (only slightly dangerous). While attending Fairview Hospital School of Nursing, riding the bus to downtown Minneapolis was an adventure in itself, strolling past the huge plate glass windows in Dayton's and Donaldson's drooling over the latest fashions and displays, riding up and down the elevators inside the stores gaping at the magnificent merchandise. One Easter, with permission to buy a dress at Dayton's, I bought a navy blue polka dot dress that made me feel like a princess.

When Leo and I married, we raised our three children in a town perfect for children—International Falls, Minnesota, where kids roamed the neighborhood in complete freedom from morning until night. A skating rink across the street prepared Allen for the Falls High Bronco and Notre Dame hockey teams, Sherry and Jayne for hockey cheerleaders and figure skaters. A small business-owner, my husband didn't take vacations from Leo's Garage, but indulged our family with weekend camping trips. From tents we progressed to trailers, heading to a campground every Friday after work, returning on Sundays. Deciding we should take a real vacation, I saved money for Disneyland. Then, Leo brought home a twenty-eight foot deluxe camping trailer. We took a vote—four for the trailer. I must admit, we had many wonderful weekends in the new trailer.

And then . . . the kids grew up and we stopped camping. Allen and Sherry were out of college and married, Jayne was off to college. My traveling increased.

Chapter 2
Caribbean Adventures
1976

"What a perfect Easter Sunday!" Lying on the deck of a Caribbean sailboat, I chanted to myself with each dip of the waves, "Per-fect East-er Sun-day."

When Marcelle first invited me to go to the Caribbean for three weeks in 1976 I immediately refused. "I don't have time to take such a long vacation." Marcelle, a petite Frenchwoman from Quebec, taught piano, dance, and exercise; I was one of the first to join her health club. Her persistent coaxing convinced me and we both became so excited, our husbands, Leo and Guy, decided to join us. With Leo and Guy planning to stay only a week, the four of us flew to the island of St. Thomas.

The week flew by. As the day approached for our husbands to leave, I longed to go home too. We'd explored St. Thomas, soaked up sunshine. I told Leo, "I can't sunbathe for two more weeks." Refusing to release me from our vacation, Marcelle promised: "We'll take turns choosing activities. And we'll treat the two weeks as a spa."

Unbelievable! Marcelle became my personal trainer. Waking early, she quietly read until my eyelids fluttered. Thrusting her book aside the instant I opened an eye, she'd spring out of bed ready to exercise. Sleepily, I followed her routine of yoga, stretches, and calisthenics. She allowed us only one meal a day, but, whether it was lunch or dinner, we dined at luxurious places, sampling extravagant Caribbean seafood. Occasionally, we split sinful desserts (usually a decadent chocolate treat). One day, seeing pictures of the notorious ferocious pirate, Blackbeard, we chose Blackbeard's Castle as an exciting restaurant to try.

Indeed, it was exciting! The non-English speaking driver nodded his head when we told him our destination. The drive seemed excessively long, with houses disappearing as the dirt road narrowed. Our tension thickened as the foliage grew thicker.

Leaning over the seat, Marcelle asked, "Are we nearly there?" He didn't answer. She whispered, "Does he think we're rich Americans? Is he kidnapping us?" My stomach clenched as I thought of my family, worrying, waiting to hear from me. Our families wouldn't be able to raise enough money! Making the sign of the cross, I prayed they wouldn't kill us. Trying not to look scared, Marcelle grabbed my hand. "I know we'll be okay. He probably took the longest route to get more money."

"There it is!" Marcelle shouted. I put my hand over my racing heart and flopped back on the seat. We nearly fell out of the car when it stopped. Inside Blackbeard's Castle, we dropped into chairs with relief. Marcelle said, "My hands are still shaking."

Gulping ice water while waiting for our wine, Marcelle casually asked, "What was your maiden name?" In our small town, everyone knows everyone from one generation to the next, but Marcelle was a "newcomer."

"St. Pierre."

Marcelle jumped up from her chair, knocking it over. "What? That's my maiden name! We're sisters!" Marcelle danced around the table to hug me.

I blurted, "My dad's ancestors lived on St. Pierre Island in Quebec. They came from Paris in the 1600s. We have to be related!" As soul-sisters, our vacation was even sweeter. Jubilantly (and bravely), we ordered octopus to mark this momentous special occasion. To our surprise, it tasted like chicken.

Reading by the pool under whispering palm trees, balmy morning breezes stirring up the scent of flowers, made me realize how delicious it is to have a relaxing vacation. When I became restless, I slipped into the pool, using it as therapy for a knee I'd injured while cross-country skiing the weekend before leaving for St. Thomas. On an icy hill, one ski got stuck and I did the splits. (Before leaving on my ski trip, Marcelle warned me not to get hurt. *Oops!*) The water therapy improved my knee, the brace I wore not only helped my knee, it brought attention and sympathy as I limped around St. Thomas.

Marcelle finally gave in to my cajoling to go sailing. Wandering the marina, we found a charter boat crewed by a young American couple, Dick and Susan. Tall, thin, and tanned, they were the epitome of the sail boaters I'd watched and envied while eating breakfast with Leo every morning at the marina. Spread eagled on the deck, rocking with the waves, soaking up sun and saltwater—up and down, sun and water, up and down. I clung to ropes and dug my heels down to keep from rolling off the curved deck into the sea. Trade winds sent us skimming over the shimmering blue water. Yes, a perfect Easter Sunday!

Lost in my private paradise, I didn't notice Marcelle disappear. When I went below for lunch, she was lying in a bunk, seasick, weakly shaking her head no to eating and snorkeling. Susan helped me into the snorkeling gear. Feeling like an alien sea creature, I struggled to get down the ladder wearing long flippers and fell off in a belly flop. I floated with my face in the water until jagged coral reefs jutting up seemed dangerously close to scraping my belly. I stiffened and sank Thrashing wildly, I surfaced again.

Schools of fish, bright, shiny, and slimy, swam below me, beside me, above me. Without my glasses, I worried I might blindly bump into a dangerous fish. The snorkel mask fogged up, water seeped in, and I gave up. Climbing up the boat ladder with trembling legs, I welcomed a helping hand from Captain Dick.

Sailing home in the rosy sunset, my skin felt hot and dry. Wearily, I stumbled to our hotel room. My chilled body shivered and shook. "Teeth really do chatter!" I thought, surprised.

Marcelle quickly recovered from her sea-sickness on land. Concerned, she tried to run a cool bath for me, but the water stayed lukewarm. Grabbing the ice bucket, she said, "I'll go get ice."

I lay shivering under covers, moaning, wondering why Marcelle wasn't back, worrying I might not survive. Where did she go? I sobbed with relief when Marcelle finally dashed into the room. "I'm so sorry. I raced through the halls begging for ice cubes. I even ran to the hotel across the street. This is all I could get." Tipping the bucket, a few ice cubes lazily floated into the lukewarm water before disappearing.

The bath offered little relief. Nauseated, weak, and dehydrated, I willingly accepted the aspirin and valium Marcelle prescribed from her purse. Never having taken a valium, I didn't know whether the pill or the sunburn would kill me, but I desperately prayed, "Please let me go home to my family," until the valium knocked me out. In the morning, I moved my singed body gingerly, surprised and grateful to be alive. "Thank you, God!"

Marcelle was relieved. "You were beet red. Your pain brought tears to my eyes."

My sunburn healed, I arrived back home tan and slim. To my astonishment, my personal trainer "sister" had trimmed me down to fit into her itty bitty yellow bikini.

Love of travel replaced housecleaning as my favorite vacation choice.

Chapter 3
The Ironing Board—*Five Generations*

Gen I
A long association,
The Ironing Board and I.
Standards are high.

Grandma Dina, early in the century,
Took in washing and ironing
To earn a living.

Grandma Dina
Had no education
For any other occupation.

Grandma's washing machine
Had a handle
To turn manually.

Grandma's iron
Black and heavy,
Not shiny electric.

Gen II
In Mama's time
Women devoted their lives
To being good housewives.

Mama's washing machine
Used electricity,
But still . . . a wringer to feed.

Twin boards in the kitchen
When I was ten.
Learned ironing basics then.

With a hiss of steam,
Fresh scent released
Of air-dried clean.

The smell of starch.
Clothes sprinkled precise
And rolled up tight.

Gen III
In my own home
Automatic washer / dryer,
A spray iron much lighter.

My Ironing Board and I
Had starch that sprayed . . .
We used it rarely.

On my Ironing Board,
A parade of clean clothing
Reviewing week's happenings.

I received an education
But not expectation
To have an occupation.

Behind my Ironing Board,
I ponder pressing problems
Of working mothers.

Magazines monthly rave:
Working mothers damage families
Shamefully grave.

Gen IV
Fourth generation
Wearing wrinkle-free
Ignore ironing board need.

No Ironing Board necessary
When they marry.
Tradition dismissed.

Gen V
New age— embraced.
Technology engaged,
Facebook, Twitter, and texting reign.

Chapter 4
Canning Conversations
1970s

Grandma Dina and my parents instilled the work ethic in me. However, my choice was *not* domesticity, but working outside the home.

My sisters-in-law followed the rule that when gardens produce, it's time to can the bounty. My husband claims he had to sneak into the garden to eat fresh peas and carrots because his mother canned them for winter. With twelve children, providing food was important.

Canning conversations dominated fall gatherings at the Karsnia farm. It was a competition! Each one bragged about how many quarts of pickles, pints of green beans, etc. filled their pantries. Everyone agreed they loved listening to popping Kerr lids. They all had stories about meeting bears in the berry patch.

Nobody wanted to talk about how fast I could type.

Slipping into the family as a non-Catholic, as a working mother, and as a non-canner, I'm not sure which mortal sin was the most offensive. After my in-laws realized their mistake, daughters-in-law had the canning clause added to their Catholic vows, I promise to love, honor, obey—and can.

Wanting to feel included, I planned a canning day. I knew the basics because Mama had trained me as her canning assistant. However, I'd preferred cuddling in my favorite chair with my nose in a book rather than over a kettle of boiling water on a hot August day.

Canning fruits and vegetables with skins involves a process called *blanching*—putting them in boiling water to help slip off the skins. This year, I'm canning tomatoes because I had the battle of beets last year. Sometimes the beet would pop out of the slippery skin so fast it would plop onto the floor with a red splatter. Other times, I needed a paring knife to part the beet from its skin. Either way, my fingers were stained and singed from skinning.

Two years ago, I canned pickles. Simple, my sisters-in-law said. "Just scour the garden dirt off the cucumbers, stuff them into the jar. Pour pickle syrup over, pop on the lids." I stuck to the kitchen floor from spilled syrup while I stood counting the pinging of popping lids. But it didn't matter if they pinged or not, the pickles weren't crispy. I blamed their softness on city water because the others had chemical-free well water.

Anyway, after hours of squeezing off their skins, my lovely red tomatoes were bruised and battered, half their original size, and squished into jars. The sink was heaped with tomato debris. The garbage disposal started groaning and grinding. And stopped. Flipping the switch didn't restart the overworked machine. I dug slimy tomato skins out of the disposal onto newspapers, stuffed leaking newspapers into the garbage. Rivulets of tomato juice dripped down from the counter tops onto the floor.

My daughter, Sherry, home from her teen-age activity, paused in the doorway, and doubled over with laughter. She stopped laughing when she had to assist me in cleaning up the chaos. "Please, Mom, don't ever can anything again." I promised. Opening a can of Green Giant is cheaper, neater, cleaner, and a time saver!

Chapter 5
Tricky Squash
1997

My friends made me promise to write a cookbook when I retired from Boise. Laughs about my squash episode prompted their request for the "original" recipes I created.

My family shuddered whenever I tried new recipes from Good Housekeeping. Sherry, who received the title Miss Betty Crocker in Falls High School (a surprise because I had no idea she knew how to cook), remembers, "Your substitutions made the recipes fail." Well, I saw no reason to run to the store for one or two ingredients when I was short on time.

One crisp fall day, Leo was on the deck with our four-year-old grandson, Adam, shucking corn. Adam had helped Grandpa Leo pick fresh produce from Uncle Jerry's garden. Adam's parents, Sherry and Jim, were coming for Sunday dinner. Busy in the kitchen, I appreciated how much easier it is to cook squash since the invention of the microwave: prick with a fork, zap it, slice it, slather with butter and brown sugar, pop it into the oven. Picking out a second small squash, I pricked, nuked, and sliced. *Oops.*

I sauntered out to the deck. "Leo, I made a little mistake. I cooked the watermelon."

"You cooked the watermelon?"

"It looked like a squash."

Adam said, "Grandma, I want some watermelon."

"Sure, Adam. You can have some watermelon. We just have to wait for it to cool off."

Taking Adam's hand, we skipped into the kitchen. "You know, Adam, most grandmas don't bother cooking the watermelon. But I cooked it special for you." Adam's Grandma Gertie is an excellent cook, I needed to do damage control. I sang, "Nothin' says lovin' like watermelon from the microwave oven!"

Adam loved the cooled watermelon.

I didn't have enough flops for a whole cookbook, so I collected favorite recipes from family and friends with a biographical snapshot about our relationships, adding the subtitle, *A Historical Collection of Cooks*. It was a best seller hot off my computer. Some cooks are still using recipes—and some are still laughing.

European Visits

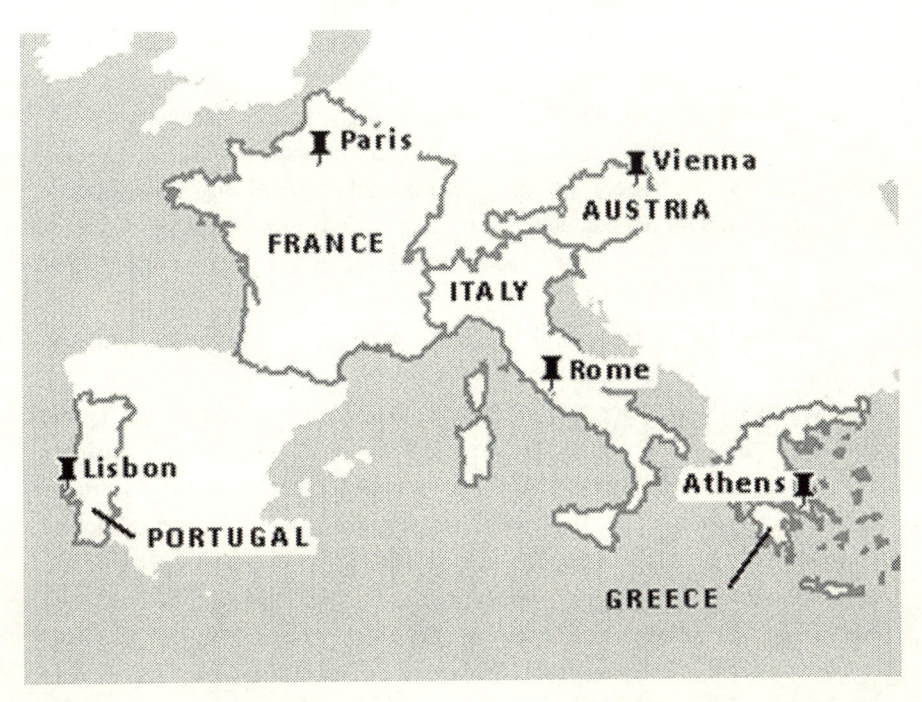

Chapter 6
Portuguese Surprises
March 1981

Apparently I infected Jayne, my younger daughter, with the travel bug. She chose a trip to Portugal with Rainy River Travel Club for her high school graduation. Delighted, I agreed it was a perfect gift because she would need a chaperone—me!

The hotel staff at Hotel Dom Carlos in Lisbon treated us royally. The Portuguese have to rank among the friendliest people in the world. Desk clerks, managers, bellboys swarmed around us, bowing and smiling, making us feel welcome. They were especially attentive to Jayne, the youngest on the trip, and I received special smiles too. Aahhh! Portuguese men!

Most of the people on the tour immediately took naps. Jayne and I dropped our luggage in our room, ready to investigate Lisbon. Lu, an experienced traveler a few years older than me, took us under her motherly wing and taught us tricks about traveling. "Each country is famous for special items. Look for Portuguese pottery and delicate embroidered items. Leather in Portugal is a must." I didn't know I should have researched "what to buy." Jayne and I had a wonderful time choosing a Baptismal dress for my first two grandchildren; both my daughter, Sherry, and Allen's wife, Kip, were expecting in June. A pair of high tan leather boots, soft as butter, found me. Tired after hitting the shops, Lu led us to the Ritz: "Always look for the best hotels if you need to use a restroom. Saunter in as though you're a guest or go in for lunch." Now, when I clean my cupboards, I find an ashtray from Lisbon Ritz. Lu insisted the ashtray came with lunch. However, luxury hotels are not always available, as you will discover in "Experiencing the Facilities."

Growing up in a small town without any big buildings, I had gaped at the magnificence of Dayton's department store in Minneapolis. Now, I gaped in awe at the massive, centuries-old, opulent buildings. Most

Americans are astounded at how well European buildings have been preserved.

Yet, leaving the city of Lisbon was a trip back in time. Traveling one hundred miles to Fatima on narrow, winding roads, decades disappeared. Simple wooden crosses dotted the countryside between small villages and small farms growing scraggly crops. There were no cars, only donkeys and horses pulling wooden carts filled with hay. Sitting in the back of a Gypsy-like wagon with yellow wheels, several men grinned and waved as we passed. In another, a wife dressed in black, a kerchief tied around her chin, sat dangling her legs over the back of the cart.

The rural countryside didn't prepare us for the splendid Basilica de Fatima. The villagers verge on poverty, but they worship in elaborate churches filled with valuable treasures. Walking up to the Basilica, Jayne and I paused at a small chapel to light a candle. Suddenly, we both were on our knees with tears running down our cheeks. I felt enveloped by an almost palpable spiritual presence. Unexpectedly, I wanted to know more about Fatima.

Reverently entering the magnificent Basilica de Fatima, I felt less self-conscious about my tears when I saw other women wiping their eyes. Kneeling in prayer, I realized why so many older, Catholic women were on this tour—destination, Fatima.

We'd grumbled that the souvenir stands seemed distasteful, but they help the villagers survive, and I bought a book about Fatima. Growing up Lutheran, I hadn't been steeped in the story. In 1917 while shepherding their sheep, three young cousins insisted they saw an apparition of a "lady dressed in white." Identified as Virgin Mary, she visited the children several times, making prophecies. Thousands of people were witnesses at her last apparition, "The Miracle of the Sun"— claiming that the sun danced. Thousands continue to make pilgrimages to the famous site.

I learned that Lisbon is one of the oldest cities in Europe—older than London, Paris, and Rome. According to archaeologists, there are Phoenician influences dating back to 1200 B.C. In Alfama, the oldest district of Lisbon, we climbed up stone steps to wander through a labyrinth of crooked streets lined with tall, tilted houses, looking as they did in the Middle Ages. Above our heads, laundry flapped from clotheslines on the rooftops. Sadly, Alfama has become the poorer district of Lisbon; the former colorful houses need paint and repairs.

On the Lisbon coast along the Atlantic Ocean, we visited fabulous resort towns. Sintra is famous for Queluz, the Royal Palace of Portugal, which is described as an "exquisite Portuguese Versailles." Estoril has remains of Roman villas dating back to the first millennium. Cascais, a poor fishing village in the twelfth century, is now a favorite beach for rich jet-setters.

Rushing off the bus for a bathroom break in the little fishing village of Nazare, the driver pointed to stairs going under the street. Scrunched together in a line on the stairs, we heard fellow traveler Marian yell, "More than one square." A short, chubby man, a black beret on his bald head, was planted in the middle of the doorway clutching a roll of toilet paper, guarding the dank hole in the wall. We weren't allowed past him without dropping coins into his palm, then he tore off one or two squares of toilet paper, our passport into one of the two small stalls. Outside again, we giggled about how he'd scowled at us, scolding with a Portuguese tirade when we insisted on more squares.

On Nazare's sandy beach, one of the finest on Portugal's coast, fishermen sat mending their nets among colorful, wooden boats. I envisioned Jesus walking among his disciples in a similar scene, picking out his disciples.

A monument declares Cabo da Roca as Europe's westernmost place. Fascinated by the vast blue vistas of sky and water, with Atlantic Ocean waves crashing against the high rocky cliffs, I agreed with a Portuguese poet's description of Cabo da Roca as the place "where the land ends and the sea begins."

But it didn't feel poetic when our lives almost ended over that sea! At Portugal's Azores Islands, a fueling stop about one thousand miles off the Portuguese coast, our plane started down—swooped back up. The pilot announced, "Sorry, the wind was too strong for us to land,"

Perhaps it was our renewed faith from Fatima that kept us calm. Women pulled rosary beads out of purses or hastily unpackaged new Fatima rosaries. Catholics fingered their beads mouthing, "Hail Mary, full of grace . . ." Tension crackled as the plane circled around again, bouncing, battling the high gusts of wind. Squeezing my beads, I held my breath, waiting . . .

Again—down and up. Murmurs of fear followed the pilot's announcement, "Well, folks, we'll give it one more try. Hopefully, we can land before we run out of fuel." Rosary beads clicked. Thankfully, God listened to our prayers storming heaven.

Everyone cheered and clapped when the wheels hit the ground. We swarmed out of the plane like prisoners fleeing during a jail break. We learned that Azores is famous for its strong gusty winds, difficulty in landing planes is an everyday occurrence.

Jayne and I arrived home grateful to be alive and grateful for our Portuguese adventure.

Chapter 7
Roman Grandeur
March 1982

"There's the pope!" The cheers grew to a roar as Pope John Paul II came into view, waving vigorously from his popemobile.

Squeezed shoulder to shoulder with a huge crowd in St. Peter's Square, we felt privileged to be in the first outdoor audience since he was shot in May, 1981. One hundred forty saints, including St. Peter and St. Paul, welcomed us from the marble colonnade high above the square, marking it as holy ground. Vatican guards on the alert scrutinized the crowds, but the carefree pope, his round, cherubic face beaming, blithely blessed his faithful followers. In return, faces glowing with love, they screamed with delight as he rode around looking like a toddler getting his first toy car.

The Polish Pope claimed that he knew Our Lady of Fatima would keep him alive. Although he was shot four times by his would-be assassin, he visited his attacker in prison to forgive him.

As a convert to Catholicism, I was surprised at how thrilled I felt to receive his blessing, absolving my guilt about spending the money on a second trip to Europe. And in 1982, we had no idea he would be canonized as a saint in 2014.

Pope John Paul II was beatified May 1, 2011, by Pope Benedict XVI, the first step in the process for sainthood. Pope Francis, the Catholic leader following Pope Benedict, plans to canonize John Paul II, and also John XXIII, "the good pope" who convened the Vatican Council in 1960. Pope Francis's message of peace and helping the poor resonated with the world; he was named Person of the Year by *Time Magazine* in December, 2013. Good Morning America hosts Robin Roberts and Josh Elliott, while televising their interview with him at the Vatican, were visibly filled with awe and reverence while shaking hands with Pope Francis. Elliott later commented, "There was a moment of calm and peace that surrounds him—it was remarkable." Possibly more extraordinary is seeing Pope Francis featured on the February 2014 cover of *Rolling Stones* magazine, calling him "Cool Pope Francis."

Staying at Michelangelo Hotel, close to the Vatican, we often walked past the Pontifical Swiss Guards in striped uniforms. We'd smile and wave, but their eyes didn't flicker as they stood like statues holding their rifles. Wearing red, blue and gold one-piece uniforms with balloon pants and matching high boots, berets on their heads, they look almost comical. However, the guards have to meet strict requirements: Catholic, unmarried, Swiss males who had trained for the Swiss Army. The one hundred ten Swiss guards have a challenge guarding Pope Francis as he mingles freely with the crowds.

St. Peter's Basilica, the church in Vatican City, is a holy site. St. Peter was persecuted, crucified upside down, and buried there. Reverently, I touched his cool marble foot that's almost worn away from millions of people stroking it. Built in the sixteenth through seventeenth century, St. Peter's is the largest church in the world, with markings on the floor showing the size of other churches, including New York's St. Patrick's Cathedral.

Michelangelo's lavish paintings surround the entire Sistine Chapel—walls and ceiling. Listening intently to the audio, searching for the paintings on the ceiling as they were described, my neck ached from looking up. Pulling off the head phones, I rolled my head around to get out the kinks. Although we were awed by the elegant architecture, the rich paintings and statues, my friends and I weren't enthused by the excessive lavishness when millions of people live in poverty. Knowing Pope Francis's concern for the poor is a breath of fresh, humble air.

Of the many churches we toured, I loved The Basilica of Our Lady in Trastevere. The photograph in my album is captioned: "One of the finest and oldest churches in Rome, dating back to the 340s, it was the first church dedicated to Mary, Mother of Jesus. The nave is covered by a thin sheet of pure gold." I think Mary deserves to be memorialized with gold! Although she was so humble, she almost certainly wouldn't appreciate such extravagance.

Bonnie, Barb, my roommate Sue, and I skipped off to The Spanish Steps to retrace the footsteps of Audrey Hepburn and Gregory Peck; the actors made the steps famous when they starred in the 1953 romantic comedy, *Roman Holiday*. Younger people may not remember them, but suave Gregory Peck was the epitome of a Hollywood heartthrob and Audrey Hepburn my favorite actress. The widest staircase in Europe was jammed with people socializing and relaxing. I intended to climb the one hundred thirty-eight steps to Trinita dei Monti, the church at the top, but gave up trying to walk around people sprawled on the steps.

Instead, at a sunny sidewalk café, we sipped coffee and people-watched. Café Greco was established in 1760 according to the napkin in my photo album. The smiling waiters filled our coffee cups, flirted, and posed with us. This is my vision of what life would be like in Italy.

The English poet, John Keats, wasn't famous when he died at age twenty-five in 1795, but the villa where he lived by the Spanish Steps is now a museum dedicated to his memory. Sitting under a plum tree watching a nightingale, he composed *Ode to a Nightingale*. Sitting on our Rainy Lake dock, I compose poems about Rainy Lake, but (sigh) none are famous.

History came alive as I walked in ancient Rome! I told Sue, "I wish I'd known when I was in school that I'd actually see the Roman Forum and Colosseum. I'd have studied harder."

Sue read from our guidebook: "The Colosseum, a four-storied amphitheater, was built in 70-80 AD and once held fifty thousand spectators." Immediately comparing the size to hockey or football stadiums, I groaned, "Their sport was watching Christians thrown to the lions!" It felt really eerie when we toured the dark Catacombs holding thousands of bones from persecuted Christians. Barb and her husband Jim, Bonnie, Sue, and I were the only members of the group who went inside.

Bonnie and Barb both are indefatigable sightseers. Bonnie, a divorced mother working two jobs despite being diagnosed with Rheumatoid Arthritis when she was only twenty-five years old, calls herself a survivor. Ignoring painful hands, she worked for the Koochiching County Highway Department and, wearing special shoes for her misshapen feet, cheerfully waited on customers in the lounge at the Holiday Inn. Barb's black hair and sparkling black eyes are evidence of her Italian genealogy, and so are her gourmet dinners. Sue, a young and pretty dental assistant, is hoping the dentist will propose marriage. We discussed her romance many nights when we should have been sleeping.

On the day trip to Pompeii, I was flabbergasted to see ancient ruins so well preserved. Pompeii was buried in layers of volcanic ash from Mount Vesuvius when it erupted in 79 A.D., preserving everything that was buried. When Roman Emperor Augustus ruled beginning 27 B.C., brilliant engineers built extraordinary temples, villas, aqueducts, and gardens. Elaborate paintings in the houses are still bright and beautiful, but erotic, embarrassing most of us women; we tried to avoid looking at them. The men—no problem. Archaeologists estimate that there were about twenty thousand inhabitants when Mount Vesuvius erupted. Huge granite columns that once supported magnificent buildings stand pointing to the sky, embracing open air. Once a favorite vacation spot for high society Romans, now it's a favorite vacation spot for high society jetsetters.

Florence, considered one of the most beautiful cities in the world, has two famous art galleries: Uffizi Gallery and Pitti Palace. At the Uffizi Museum, *David* held me captive. I couldn't take my eyes off the sculpture that Michelangelo carved from one solid chunk of granite, capturing the strength of a man chosen by God. *David* doesn't show his age, although he lived outside for four hundred years before becoming the centerpiece inside Uffizi.

Italy's overwhelming history covers thousands of years. I dragged home thick books filled with pictures of Italy's awesome art and architecture and magnificent buildings to help me remember all I'd seen!

Traveling is a learning experience, and I've learned we live in a remarkable world!

Chapter 8
Viennese Splendor
March 1983

Halleluiah! Palm Sunday in Vienna!

Twisting, turning, gawking in awe at the glittering splendor, we walked wide-eyed through Hofburg Palace on our way to the Imperial Music Chapel. Back home at St. Thomas Aquinas Catholic Church, we make our entry into Palm Sunday Mass waving palms and singing, but here, I was taken aback to see huge pots of pussy willows decorating the chapel. However, the soprano voices and heavenly harmony of Vienna Boys Choir singing hymns of praise swirled around us with the incense. Cherubic faces, white robes, and voices like angels felt like a peek into paradise.

From heavenly angels, we visited a museum where heavenly piano music had been created. In Mozarthaus, Wolfgang Mozart's former apartment, we admired the highly polished, black grand piano on which he began composing at the age of five.

Melodious church bells were ringing when we left the apartment. Noticing our puzzled faces, a passerby stopped to say, "The Holy Door is opening in the Basilica in Rome." Simultaneously, Bonnie and I exclaimed, "We saw the Holy Door in Rome last year!" It's a beautiful door with sixteen bronze panels of Biblical scenes. It's sealed shut from the other side and is opened every twenty-five years for Jubilee Years.

I felt blessed that I had seen the pope and the holy door when, as a member of the St. Thomas Aquinas Catholic Church Worship Commission, I participated in the year-long preparation in anticipation of the Great Jubilee of 2000. Pope John Paul II opened the holy door shortly before midnight on December 24, 1999—a symbol of opening the doors of God's grace—and then celebrated midnight Mass in St. Peter's Basilica.

With my new enthusiasm for traveling, I had immediately signed up for the Rainy River Travel Club trip to Vienna with Lucy, a nurse at Boise, as my roommate. We have similar personalities, a bit serious but fun-loving. Our daughters are friends in school, and they were a camping family too. We'd often meet them at Morson Park in Canada.

Lucy and I had agreed that our inspirational Palm Sunday in Vienna was worth the price of the trip. As all mothers, we felt guilty about spending money on ourselves.

But there was more to dazzle us in the "City of Music." Horses performing in a palace seemed bizarre, but the Lipizzaner horses charmed us. Beneath shimmering crystal chandeliers in Hofburg Palace, the brilliant white stallions danced and pranced arrogantly, in perfect unison, to classical music.

The sheer beauty of the production of Romeo and Juliet at the Vienna State Opera kept us enthralled for scene after stunning scene of the classic tale about doomed lovers. I gasped when the curtain opened, illuminating *en pointe* dancers in their glittering white tutus. The voices and musicians, the twirling, leaping, and pirouettes, the costumes, sets and lighting—all held me transfixed, barely able to move a muscle. Never had I experienced anything this exquisite.

Our itinerary included a side trip to Budapest, Hungary. The Blue Danube was not blue when we crossed it on our trip to Budapest. Helga, our guide who looked as stern as her name, tried to convince us that the rainy day was to blame for the murky grey color, but we wanted to see the brilliant blue Danube of the famous song.

The cloud of gloom that hung over our group deepened when armed soldiers invaded our bus, demanded our passports and visas, then marched away with them. Helga shrugged at our protests, she could do nothing. Our documents would be held until our return to Austria. A busload of carefree tourists turned into a busload of nervous tourists.

Helga tried to divert our anger with facts about Budapest. "Budapest is one of the world's loveliest cities, one more pearl strung on the Danube necklace." Lunch in the ritzy restaurant, Hungaria, which she claimed was a former meeting place for poets and writers, did nothing to dispel the gloominess. The food was delicious and presented tastily, the chandeliers and décor glittered, but, for me, the joy of the trip had vanished at the border.

Whether it was the rain or worry, after Vienna's splendor I thought Budapest was dull and drab. In Vienna, we'd freely visited magnificent palaces, cathedrals, and museums filled with treasures. We'd viewed famous paintings in Schonbrunn Palace, and St. Stephans Church. I bought postcards of famous paintings from Kunsthistorisches Museum. Truthfully, I was too worried to enjoy Budapest's so-called wonders. Forty of us were anxious to get our passports returned.

Back at the border, soldiers forced us to wait outside in the rain while they searched the bus. Cold and frightened, I shivered uncontrollably. Finally, we were allowed to leave. Whooosh! Everyone exhaled. Safely back in Austria's Hotel Alpha, I snuggled under the covers, grateful to be in a free country.

The Sound of Music was a perfect antidote for Hungary's gloom. "The hills are alive with the sound of music" we sang, waltzing around the gazebo in Salzburg Park with snow-tipped mountains shining down at us. After our Budapest experience with soldiers, I felt the terror of the Von Trapp family trying to escape from Nazis.

On the ride back from Salzburg, Barb suggested, "The Danube was disappointing. Let's skip the 'Romantic Danube Valley' tour and take a train to Munich." Six of us enthusiastically agreed. Barb and Bonnie wasted no time in organizing this unscheduled trip. Well, maybe they forgot a few details in their rush. First, we boarded the wrong train, and then made a frantic dash to get on the right train. And—we had wine and cheese but no utensils; gutsy Barb quickly found new friends who had the price of admission to our picnic—a wine opener and a knife. Nose pressed to the window as the train traveled through the breathtaking mountain scenery, I felt nostalgic as I remembered my childhood friend, *Heidi,* who lived with her grandpa in the Swiss Alps.

Germans know how to drink beer! The picnic-style tables in Hofbrauhaus were filled with people having a grand time. Using both hands to lift my heavy mug of deliciously cold beer, my arms ached for the waitresses carrying three huge mugs in each hand or balancing several on trays as they wound their way around the tables. Bonnie, who has carried many drinks in the Holiday Inn lounge, said, "They are amazing!" Friendly German guys taught us the "chicken dance." Patiently, they showed us the moves over and over. I surprised my husband when I "chicken danced" at the next party we attended. We left Hofbrauhaus in the wee morning hours after the best beer party ever. Walking the clean, wide, and brightly-lit streets, Barb said, "I feel safer here than back home."

Packing to go home, I struggled to close my suitcase with my new Loden coat. Although green isn't my favorite color, I couldn't leave without a famous Austrian coat (per Lu's instructions.) Thanks, Lu! It coordinated beautifully with the tan leather boots I purchased in Portugal.

Chapter 9
November Phenomenon
Annual Event

The absolute opposite of a cultural experience in Vienna is a strange phenomenon in International Falls (and the entire state of Minnesota) in November. Men disappear into the woods and aren't seen again for days, or even weeks. Sons from faraway places migrate home to head to the woods. Deer season is a sacred ritual.

Boise Paper runs with skeleton crews. Vacations are awarded by seniority. Length of service is calculated to the minute. Mournful faces, looking like they lost the lottery, man the machines.

To the chagrin of local employees, corporate headquarters is located in a different state and unaware that this is a three-week "holy holiday." Productivity is expected to continue as though it were ordinary time. Customers expect on-time deliveries.

In local sporting stores, cash registers zing. Ka-ching! Blaze orange outfits, rifles, and four-wheeler sales surge. Gas pumps whirl dollar signs as overloaded trucks guzzle fuel. Ka-ching! Men swarm through checkout counters with overflowing shopping carts, buying groceries that could feed a family for a year. Liquor, wine, and untold cases of beer are bought in wholesale lots. Ka-ching! Occasionally, a hunter remembers to buy a little gift for the wife.

Women's stress levels vary depending on age: New brides weep. Young mothers plead. Wives with independent children wait with glee. PMS in all age groups is prevalent prior to the hunters' exodus. Particularly since, in the preceding weeks, husbands have focused on preparations for deer season.

Deer season covertly begins in October. The male mind has no room for other trivia when focused on action plans: Weekend trips to the shack to check on necessary repairs. Trips to make those repairs. Supplies to buy. Sighting in the rifle. Target practice. Looking at new guns. Tales told about last year's hunt—and the year before, and the year before . . . The deer they shot and those they did not . . . No deer stories are forgotten.

Old deer stories tend to make the wife share in the hunter's fever. Her enthusiasm for the day of departure increases with each new pile of stuff stacked throughout the house. Big boots and blaze orange jackets decorate the living room.

Insignificant events might trigger a mighty battle. Perhaps she walks into a freshly scrubbed kitchen, sniffs. It doesn't smell like Mr. Clean. It smells like oil. Rifle parts glistening with oil leak on clean counters. Self-control snaps. She leaps at her husband, yanks at his ugly, scraggly beard grown for the deer shack.

Finally, duffel bags and boxes of groceries are loaded into trucks. Trucks hauling trailers of expensive toys pull out of driveways. Some women (or maybe just me) dance with the vacuum through an uncluttered house. Others catapult out the door, tires squealing all the way to their favorite coffee shop.

Women wearing wide grins gather en-masse at restaurants, fashion shows, and craft shows. Pointing purses, women hunt sales. Carloads of women speed to larger towns with bigger malls and theaters. I thoroughly enjoy the time as a vacation at home. Luckily, one year I flew to Las Vegas with MaryVon and Shirley. Gladys Knight and the Pips were outstanding, but at Liberace's performance everyone went wild. Chauffeured onstage in a Rolls-Royce, "Mr. Showmanship" stepped out of the white convertible with a smile as dazzling as his bling.

Unfortunately, negative events sometimes intervene to destroy the bliss. Murphy's Law decrees that if anything is going to break down, it will happen during deer season. Cars stop running, water pipes burst, basements flood, appliances stop working, or the furnace acts up. Children have tantrums; teenagers extend curfews.

I thought I'd paid my dues through the years, but one year Murphy remembered me. Our first winter blizzard blindsided me with a power outage. A powerless garage opener held me prisoner. I spent the night huddled in the bathroom with candles for warmth.

That reminds me, I have to review my evacuation plan so I don't miss any festivities. Check flashlights. Buy batteries. Watch weather reports. At sight of *first* snowflake, open garage door.

Chapter 10
Flying Free, Jayne and Me
1986

I felt like Cinderella during a dream year of travel with my daughter Jayne. Instead of Saturday housework after a week at the office, I'd wake up in a glamorous hotel room in a big city, transported into a weekend of luxury instead of drudgery, a weekend to share new experiences with my daughter.

After graduating from St. Scholastica College, Jayne took a job in the finance department at Republic Airlines. She flew somewhere—free—nearly every weekend in 1985. I had the privilege of flying with her—free—five times. (Unfortunately, the other travel expenses were pricey, but the trips—priceless.) Traveling with Jayne provided me with an unexpected opportunity to discover America. We explored Atlanta, Boston, New York City, San Francisco, and Washington D.C. I felt the jolt of an abrupt stop when Northwest acquired Republic and Jayne took another job without travel benefits for Mom.

Atlanta was first on our itinerary because we'd never visited the Deep South. Surprised at the traffic and the skyscrapers as Jayne drove our rental car into the busy city, we became a little intimidated. Instead of touring the city, we drove to Stone Mountain, noticing that the trees looked different than our piney forests. Stone Mountain, shaped in the form of a huge dome, is alleged to be the largest exposed piece of granite in the world. Three famous Confederate men are carved in it: Stonewall Jackson, Robert E. Lee, and Jefferson Davis. After walking on the mountain, communing with southern nature, we returned to Atlanta to find the highly-recommended Aunt Pitty Pat's Restaurant. Sipping mint juleps in a rocking chair on the porch at Aunt Pitty Pat's Restaurant, we felt like real southerners. But skip the grits!

* * *

I left my heart in San Francisco—and a few years, too. Roaming with my twenty-two-year-old daughter made me feel young and adventurous. One midnight, I was hanging on the outside of the famous San Francisco cable car! I gripped the bars until my hands cramped, but I did it!

Lombard Street is "the crookedest street in the world," a "corkscrew" with eight sharp turns that enabled horses to go up and down. On Haight Street, colorful Victorian houses built in mid-1800 are snuggled wall to wall, grassless, but beautifully landscaped with shrubs and flowers. In the 1960s, there were about two hundred thousand flower children living among the flowers, but now in 1990 the area appears sedately middle-aged. I was busy raising three children during that time, shocked at such an irresponsible lifestyle.

San Francisco is built on forty-four hills. The rich and famous built mansions on Nob Hill, one of the original "Seven Hills" until it was destroyed in the 1906 earthquake and fire. (While I was on a business trip to California, I experienced tremors in the Sacramento airport during the 1989 San Francisco earthquake. Wondering why I was suddenly so dizzy, I hung onto the table to keep from falling off my chair. Voices yelled, "It's an earthquake!" However, passengers were loaded onto planes. Mine was diverted to a military base, where we waited for buses to come and transport us to Orange County. In that pre-cell phone era, we had no information about what was happening. I didn't reach my hotel until after midnight, and not expecting my family to hear about a California earthquake, I didn't call them. However, I didn't take into account that, with the third game of the World Series starting at 5:00 p.m., the quake was broadcast immediately, causing panic in my family. *Oops!)*

At the top of Nob Hill, we had a grand view of San Francisco Bay and Fisherman's Wharf, enticing Jayne and me down to the famous shops. Fisherman's Wharf was lively with jugglers, acrobats, and mimes; we often stopped to watch them as we shopped in Ghirardelli Square, Pier 39, and the Cannery Shopping Center.

From Pier 33, we took an Alcatraz Cruise boat to the former federal prison. Inside and out, Alcatraz is stark, dreary, and depressing. Walking down hallways past the regular cells was creepy enough, but when they slammed us inside solitary confinement cells, I felt frantic. The door closed with a bang as loud as a gun at close range. I was glad to get out of there! Scrambling over "The Rock" on our way back to the boat, imagining soldiers with rifles in the tower, I wondered whether any prisoners had escaped. (I learned that nobody had successfully escaped in the penitentiary's twenty-nine-year history, but out of the thirty-six prisoners who attempted to escape, six had been shot and killed. I think the hope of freedom was worth the risk of death.)

Other favorite activities: Wandering the soothing, peaceful paths of precise beauty in Japanese Tea Garden. Driving across the San Francisco Bridge to Marin County to lunch at an outdoor café in the sun. On an all-day Napa Valley Tour of vineyards we were given lessons in the proper way to sample wine, swishing it in the mouth and spitting it out. Instead of swishing, I swallowed. Why waste free wine?

After a day of sightseeing and shopping, plunking down on stools in Buena Vista inhaling the aroma of coffee, watching bartenders who serve over two thousand cups a day, and savoring Irish Coffee topped with whipped cream is a delicious way of winding down.

* * *

In New York City, bagels and coffee at a deli each morning powered us off to see famous landmarks. Sailing down the Hudson River on the Circle Line boat tour was a wonderful way to hear history lessons about the Big Apple as we stared at the impressive skyline of tall skyscrapers glittering in the sun. Approaching the Statue of Liberty with her torch held high, my throat felt tight with emotion as I thought about the millions of immigrants seeing her for the first time. I thought about my husband's grandfather who left Ireland in 1888, determined to own land and have the right to vote in America, and how proud he was of achieving his dreams. While writing *A Bit of Irish Gold*, my first book, I felt like I took the journey with him.

My daughters came with me on my first trip to New York in 1970. Before leaving home, a shooting in the subway had been on the news, making Sherry and Jayne as nervous as me. Visiting my friend, Tammy, in her apartment in Greenwich Village, she scoffed, "The subway is perfectly safe. There are only a few shootings each year." On this trip in 1986, Jayne and I are still jumpy about riding the subway, and when we popped up the subway steps in Harlem by mistake, we looked around, immediately turned around, and scampered back down to catch another train.

It tugged at our hearts to see homeless huddled in doorways, heads resting on bundles of belongings; to see women wandering the streets pushing all their possessions in grocery carts; to see disabled homeless holding out cups to collect coins for survival. I happily went home to trees and flowers, to the solitude and serenity of blue lake and splashing waves.

* * *

Washington D.C. was another dream trip. Pinching myself, I said, "Jayne, I can't believe we're here, walking on Pennsylvania Avenue in front of the White House." Joining the line to tour the White House, we nervously put down our purses for security to check. Peering into elegant rooms that entertain kings and diplomats, we were careful not to trespass past the ropes. Reverently peeking into Lincoln's Bedroom, I hoped that dignitaries who had the privilege of sleeping there would be inspired to emulate him.

Later, looking up at Lincoln's statue gazing solemnly down at us from his giant chair on Washington Mall, I recalled his stirring words in the Gettysburg Address: ". . . all men are created equal . . ." I can't help wishing that modern politicians lived by his principles. He also said, "A new beginning under God." Why are we allowing a minority to insist we take "In God we trust" off our money and out of the Pledge of Allegiance and not allowing prayer in schools? Lincoln must be devastated. "Lincoln, we need you back!"

At the Vietnam Veterans Memorial, Jayne and I tearfully observed visitors clutching flowers, placing them by the names of loved ones who lost their lives in America's longest war. The first veterans died in May, 1959, and the last in 1975. In 1984, a statue of Three Soldiers was added, portraying an African American, Hispanic and Caucasian. It's pointed toward the wall, as though they are honoring the fifty-eight thousand fellow soldiers who sacrificed their lives.

The Smithsonian has extraordinary exhibits, but when I saw Charles Lindbergh's plane prominently displayed in the Air and Space Museum, I felt a sense of pride and stood there a long time. Minnesota claims Lindbergh because he grew up in Little Falls, Minnesota. In 1927,

"Lucky Lindy" flew non-stop from New York, landing his silver plane in Paris thirty-three hours safely after fighting "fog, icing, and sleep deprivation." But his luck didn't last. In the "Crime of the Century" in 1932, twenty-month old Charles Augustus Lindbergh, Jr. was kidnapped and killed, so we Minnesotans hold the family in our hearts.

The Smithsonian is overwhelming! We raced from one museum to the next. Pausing in the American History Museum, we admired the display of gowns worn by First Ladies to the presidential inaugurations and balls, a fascinating display of fashion through the years. To me, Jackie Kennedy was the loveliest of them all.

D.C. subways were spotless and we felt completely safe, unlike New York. I appreciated the cleanliness, but not the posted signs warning not to bring in food or drink. Starting out early each morning, I really wanted a cup of coffee in my hand!

* * *

We flew to Boston in the lap of luxury, upgrading to first class for our final trip. With tablecloths draped on our trays, the flight attendant served hors d'oeuvres of grapes and cheese, a salad, and a chicken breast. First class service was great in 1986! Looking out the window as the plane nosed down, I saw only a watery runway. Leaning back in the seat, closing my eyes and crossing my fingers, I prayed until the wheels landed with a thump.

Boston is a living history lesson. Boston Commons, established in 1634, is the oldest public park in the country. We were pleasantly surprised on that sunny Saturday morning to walk out of Park Plaza Hotel to see Boston Commons right across the street. It was Labor Day weekend and college students were having a blast propelling swan boats in the pond. John Paget introduced the swan boat in 1877 and his descendants have added to the fleet of boats, a popular way to enjoy twenty-four acres of nature in the middle of a busy metropolitan city.

Bill, our tall and lanky Boston College student working as a Bean Trolley tour guide, filled us with facts about Paul Revere's talents—an American silversmith, an early industrialist, a patriot in the American Revolution—and the father of sixteen children. Paul instructed the sexton of North Church to use lanterns, "one if by land, two if by sea," to warn the colonists. Before galloping off on his midnight ride after seeing two lanterns, Revere had to cross the Charles River by rowboat and slip past a British warship before galloping off on his legendary ride. History might be different if he'd been caught!

In Quincy Market we squeezed through crowds buying food and souvenirs on our way to Old South Church. The church is called the "sanctuary of freedom" because about one hundred men disguised as Mohawk Indians went war whooping around the church before joining the Boston Tea Party at the waterfront. At the Tea Party Museum, while watching a movie about the infamous Tea Party, we sipped tea served by a woman wearing a Colonial dress.

The USS Constitution, the oldest ship in the Navy, is surprisingly small to have won so many fierce battles. (My husband insisted on tours of the Constitution whenever we visited our son while he lived in Boston.) Sailors in Revolutionary garb giving the tour claim that Old Ironsides, built with petrified wood, went to battle forty-two times without a single loss. In the lowest level, short hammocks were strung six inches apart, with duffel bags for the seamens' personal belongings. The cat o'nine tails still hanging on the wall gave me the shivers! How many sailors were punished with nine lashes from that?

Exploring the fashionable neighborhoods on Beacon Hill, we joined the line waiting to go into the famous TV bar, Cheers. Inside, we stopped abruptly. Cameras had given the illusion of a much bigger TV Cheers. We backed out, too disillusioned to buy a single souvenir.

In line at No Name Restaurant, supposedly the best restaurant in Boston for lobsters, we chatted with a father and son behind us. Noticing that groups of four or more were being seated while we were ignored, Jerome and Jerry asked if we wanted to join them. We were seated immediately. When Jerome asked Jayne if she was a college student, she said, "I work at Republic Airlines, but this is our last trip because I'm going to work at Cargill." Jerome said, "Well, this is a coincidence. I sold my meat company to Cargill."

We went to Harvard! Harvard Square is a kaleidoscope of coffee shops, book and craft stores, boutiques, sidewalk cafes, and lively students. My favorite place was Longfellow House on Brattle Street, where Longfellow sat "under the spreading chestnut tree" to write his poems. He wrote *Paul Revere's Ride,* one of my favorite poems, now even more meaningful after learning more about Paul. Before leaving

Longfellow's house, I reverently stroked the polished banister on the stairway hoping to spark some of his *writing muse* into my fingers.

* * *

After seeing more of the United States of America than I'd seen in my lifetime, I saw even more! Leo and I drove to Billings, Montana and joined our friends, Don and Sally, to drive to Vancouver, British Columbia for Vancouver Expo 86. The theme of the Canadian Expo was "Transportation and Communication: World in Motion—World in Touch." I was fascinated with Japan's bullet train and other futuristic exhibits. On our way to Vancouver, on a Canadian golf course in Lethbridge, Alberta, Leo made a hole-in-one. On the way home, we stopped in Banff National Park, Canada's oldest national park, established in 1885 in the Rocky Mountains. Our husbands refused to pay the price of a room in Chateau Lake Louise, which looks like a castle, but Sally and I wandered around admiring the elegance. The Chateau is nestled in a fairyland setting overlooking sparkling blue Lake Louise, surrounded by towering Rockies.

I titled my 1986 Christmas Newsletter *My Year of Travel*. A year I cherish!

Chapter 11
Superlative Shopping Excursion
1984

My friend Bonnie asked, "Do you want to go to Greece in April? Barb and I are launching our own tour company, International Tours." Of course I wanted to go to Greece with my adventurous friends! The feisty pair isn't afraid to ask questions, they demand answers, and pack as much as possible into a trip. I packed my bag!

In Athens, I realized that some women in our tour group were there primarily for a shopping extravaganza—gold, jewelry, and furs. Shopping? In Athens, home of Olympian gods and Phoenician kings and noted philosophers—a civilization born long before Christ was born. Furs? Hollywood stars wore furs and maybe a few rich elderly ladies back home in Minnesota. I was neither. Luckily, my roommate, Clari, wanted to experience Greece, too. We didn't know each other well, but we liked each other and wanted to see as much as we could.

Clari and I shivered with excitement as we walked in places formerly trod on by Greek gods. We gazed up at the Acropolis high on a rocky hill overlooking Athens. "Built before Christ," I exclaimed. "It blows my mind that some of it is still standing!"

Athens was named after Goddess Athena, and the Parthenon is the magnificent temple honoring her. Walking in the ancient Agora of Athens, the old marketplace where Socrates and his student, Plato, walked long ago, I asked Clari, "How did they get so smart when there weren't many books yet? Their wisdom has been handed down through the ages. And doctors are still taking the Hippocratic Oath; they are following some health rules that Hippocrates discovered over 2000 years ago."

We joined fur-modeling sessions in hotel rooms each evening. Proud new owners flaunted their purchases, snuggling into their coats, faces glowing before an audience relaxing on chairs and beds. Stroking the soft fur with oohhs and aahhs, we admired the silk lining luxuriously embroidered with the owner's initials.

Bonnie kept us laughing with stories about browsing through fur stores, helping others make choices. She assisted Bev in picking out a fabulous fur, far above my credit card limit. Mary's full-length mink wrapped cozily around her for warmth. Joan found a sophisticated white fur jacket. It was love at first sight for Lillian and a blue fox. Clari and I watched in wonder as they modeled coats with big price tags.

Bonnie tortured herself with those daily trips of temptation before finally being captured by a full-length Canadian raccoon. "The owner at No Name Furrier gave me a good price because so many of my friends bought furs there." Laughing, Bonnie asked, "How could I resist a sale price?" However, when the adrenaline stopped flowing, guilt took over. Trying to cheer her up, Joan said, "Those ill-fated raccoons were transported from Canada all the way to Greece to become a coat—and now you can bring them home with you. We live on the Canadian border, it'll feel like a homecoming for them." Bonnie's depression after her impulsive purchase improved after a little therapy from her amateur psychiatrists. Shrugging her shoulders, "Oh, well. Who needs to eat?"

Finally, Clari and I caved, convincing ourselves we should sample privileged shopping. "Let's pretend we're rich Americans buying furs! It'll be fun. They won't know we aren't going to buy anything."

Easily slipping into our role of pseudo-rich, Clari and I sauntered into the Hotel Grande Bretagne dining room for breakfast served by white-coated waiters before leaving on our ritzy shopping trip. Vases of fresh flowers decorated crisp white linen-clad tables set with lovely china. Staying at the elegant Hotel Grande Bretagne, constructed in 1843 and furnished with exquisite antiques, luxury oozed through our pores and we almost believed we were wealthy.

The hotel doorman looked at the business cards from Stelio and Paul, owners of Vancouver furs we'd met the night before while dining at the Hilton. He shook his head. "No go there." Summoning a cab with a raised arm and snap of his fingers, the doorman directed taxi driver Demetrius to Hydra Furs. Demetrius escorted us inside the store to personally introduce us to the sales manager, Marinos. (Does that smell like a set-up to you? Writing it now, I think it was!)

Clari and I casually shrugged into minks priced at $2,000, pirouetting in front of the mirror. On a pretend shopping trip, why not start with the best? Sitting on an elegant brocaded sofa sipping coffee in demitasse cups served from silver platters, we took turns modeling coats. Parading to the mirror, we'd giggle, "We'll be mistaken for bear cubs." (We're both short.)

Working down to the lower-priced jackets, we told Marinos, "We live in Minnesota." With an exaggerated shiver, he said, "Very cold! Need warm coat." Marinos helped us in and out of coats, flinging discarded jackets over the exquisite furniture. His smile gradually diminished as we dallied and he disappeared to help a more promising customer. Clari and I, no strangers to inattentive clerks at home, continued trying on coats.

We stayed too long and got lost in our game of pretense. We found fur jackets that screamed, "Buy me!" Clari declared, "We live in the Ice Box of the Nation. We deserve a fur coat!"

"It's our obligation as tourists in Greece," I replied.

Taking our mink jackets to the counter, our hands trembled as we handed over our credit cards. Clari asked, "May I have a beer?" We sank into soft leather chairs gulping our beer while waiting for our initials to be embroidered in our coats, our nerves shot. "What have we done? What will our husbands say?" The beer didn't help us recover from our fur coat caper.

Overcome by guilt as we carried our big boxes back to Hotel Grande, we rushed to our room. Like two kids who got caught with their hands in the cookie jar, we shoved the big boxes under our beds. Trembling, we threw ourselves on top of the beds moaning, "We can't take the coats back, they have our initials."

Glancing out the window, Clari interrupted our misery. "Look! It's the changing of the guard." We'd walked past the Presidential Guards standing at attention in front of the Presidential Palace many times. The Evzones (guards) wore black tunics belted at the waist over white kilts and leggings, velvet burgundy helmets on their heads. Leaving their miniature guardhouse, they marched like wooden marionettes. Slowly and precisely, slapping their rifles in unison, the line of soldiers turned, made a kick step, paused briefly, then marched across the square. New soldiers marched over to stand at attention in front of the diminutive guardhouse, the size of our outhouse at our hunting shack, but much prettier. The exhibition was over quickly, but the interlude revived our shattered nerves. Changing of the guard mysteriously pardoned us from our sins, releasing us for more adventures.

Athens has a population of four million people. Despite the congestion, life is an outdoor extravaganza. Greek tycoons behind sunglasses close multi-million-drachma-shipping deals where Socrates and Plato and other wise Greeks strolled in togas pondering the universe. People watchers relax over cups of coffee under café awnings.

A few times, we joined our friends to shop in the Plaka, the Old City. The Plaka is far more exciting than American malls. Shopkeepers resembling handsome brown-eyed Greek gods lounged in doorways only one step away from the narrow lanes. And they know how to treat a shopper! Enticingly, they beckoned us in from the street, quickly ushered us into the back of the store to a lounge. "Come. Have Ouzo." Have you ever been ushered into the back of an American store to sip liqueur from a tiny glass? Sorry, Sam Walton, I find that sorely lacking in Wal-mart stores.

Greek men love to flirt. They appreciate American women regardless of age. Or could American money be the lure? Who cares when we're getting charmed! In Piraeus, a headwaiter kissed Lillian's hand as he led us to a table by the harbor. In the Plaka, a shopkeeper walked us to his favorite restaurant. A jewelry store clerk escorted me to my hotel so I could get my money out of the hotel safe to pay for gold necklaces for my daughters. Talk about wanting to make a sale! American sales people—take lessons!

Clari and I were hesitating on a busy street corner when a charming young man offered to help us across the street. "What hotel you staying at?" He nodded happily when we told him Hotel Grande Bretagne. "Have you been to a Greek taverna?"

"We went to the Rago."

In a disgusted tone he said, "That's just for tourists. I'll take you to a real Greek taverna with Greek dancing." Puzzling over why he offered to escort two older women, I suddenly got it. "How much do you charge?"

Our faux Boy Scout answered: "One hundred fifty dollars. But that includes wine." Pretending to accept his offer, we arranged to meet at 9:00 p.m. in front of the post office.

Walking away, Clari laughed, "The belly dancer at the Rago last night gave Jim and Arnold the time of their lives. She enjoyed tantalizing them, twirling her tassels, shaking her dangling jewelry over them.

Arnold definitely enjoyed it, even though he got beet red when she kissed his bald head."

"Quite a treat for an eighty-year-old, but he swore us all to secrecy, worried that his wife, Eva, would find out. He felt bad that she was too sick to come on the trip. It didn't bother Barb to see the dancer prancing around Jim, but I don't think Eva would have allowed Arnold to go to the Rago if she'd been on the trip."

Clari said, "You were really surprised to see your neighbor in the restroom."

"I'm still in shock. Marilyn grew up next door to me on Ninth Street, but I haven't seen her for at least ten years. When I caught a glimpse of her in the mirror, I wasn't sure it was her. I whispered, 'Marilyn?' She turned around, shocked to see me, too."

Clari said, "She enjoyed visiting with all of us."

Our grumbling stomachs forced us into a tiny, quaint restaurant with big pots bubbling on the stove behind a counter. The tantalizing aroma of rich tomato sauce made our choice easy. We both pointed at the spaghetti with chunky bread. After making our choices, we noticed there were no other women at the small round tables. A man at the table next to us wore a black suit and a jaunty black beret. His eyes twinkled as he flirted with us while nursing his beer.

In broken English the Greek informed us that he was seventy-eight years old. "I eat here for forty years." I asked him to take our picture. He said, "You teach me to use this machine, I do it!" Instead, Clari jumped up to stand beside his table and he gave a big smile for the "machine."

He moved over to our table, anxious to talk politics. When we told him we were from Minnesota, he said, "Mondale from Minnesota. I like Jesse Jackson—he is black. Carter was a good man. Nixon was good, but . . ." He made a gesture that inferred Nixon was crooked."

As we stood to leave, our friend put on his black beret and grabbed his cane. With difficulty, he managed to stand with both hands on the handle of his cane, his back bent almost double. As I pointed the camera at him, his crooked back straightened, he stood tall and proud for the "machine."

We were sad to leave Greece: Greek history going back to Socrates Greek hospitality, Greek shopkeepers serving beer and ouzo. Yes, and those Greek shopkeepers who forced us to buy furs. Our group teased

Clari and me: "You insisted you weren't interested, then you sneak off and come back with mink!"

I blamed them. "Every night we watched you flaunting your furs—you tempted us to go on a pretend shopping trip. And the mink captured us!"

Still remorseful over buying furs, the long flight gave us time to find reasons justifying our purchases. Picturing husbands' reactions, we brainstormed how to present our coats to them. I said, "We can't take the coat out of our closet and casually slip it on. Even a husband would know his wife didn't own a fur coat."

But after a long absence, we creatively modeled our furs and our marriages survived the mink.

Chapter 12
Cruising the Aegean Sea
1984 Greece trip continued

Island hopping in the Aegean Sea began with the very beginning of civilization. Our trip to Greece included a three-day cruise to the Greek islands. Sitting in the port of Piraeus in Athens, our cruise ship, Constellation, looked huge

As our ship approached Mykonos, we watched fat, round windmills come into view, juxtaposed against square white buildings carved into the hills. Bright red and blue doors and shutters shone against the white stucco walls. Painters and photographers love capturing the beauty of Mykonos.

Trudging up many levels of steps winding around tiers of homes, through cobblestoned walkways enclosed with square walls, we stopped to admire flourishing pots of flowers on the walkways and walls. Catching whiffs of tantalizing cooking smells, we peeked into open doors of small kitchens where women were stirring pots on their stoves. In cafes, men were drinking beer. Yeah, women cook while men relax.

Leaving our group browsing through the tourist traps, Clari and I climbed up toward four thatched windmills at the top of the hill. Hundreds of steps later, both of us puffing, we finally reached the windmills. By then, it was dark and we could do nothing but congratulate ourselves that we had the fortitude to reach the top before turning around.

Night descended swiftly, and we hurried through the dark maze of streets in a panic. When a young man popped out of the night, we breathlessly asked for directions to the harbor; with typical Greek friendliness, he led us through the narrow, winding, cobblestoned streets. There wasn't a blade of grass but colorful pots overflowed with flowers. Carefully, we side-stepped dog and cat droppings.

In a Greek Orthodox Church lit by gleaming crystal chandeliers, parishioners were chanting evening prayers, with a cloud of incense floating outside. We squeezed around women dressed in long black dresses visiting on their way home from church.

Clambering into the last boat, we took deep breaths of the balmy air, trying to calm down. At the Constellation, I hesitated before attempting the gangplank. I'd discovered when we boarded in the port of Piraeus that the narrow walkway swinging with each step is a difficult balancing trick, especially loaded down with luggage. Now, I clutched my purse tightly to my chest for fear of dropping it into the dark water. Grabbing the rope railing, thrusting my body forward, I climbed up the slippery metal steps swaying over the sea.

Safely on board, Clari and I stumbled breathlessly to our gray shoebox called a stateroom to change for the Mexican buffet. Hours later, after dinner and an evening of 'Fun and Games' we flopped into our hard narrow cots. I said, "The crew works hard to keep us entertained but it would have been fun to stay longer in Mykonos." Aahhh, Mykonos!

Disembarking in Rhodes the next morning, we were met by a camel and his Greek owners. Yes, with Turkey visible across the sea, a camel was conveniently parked for picture-taking. Several of us stopped to pose for pictures. I squinted up at the tall camel. "How do I get up there? Is he going to kneel down?" The Greek camel tender set a small ladder in front of me. Carefully climbing up, I plunked down between the camel's humps. After the pictures were taken, the peasants briskly became business people. With improved English, they handed us "Foto Kamel" tickets, promising that the pictures would be delivered to the ship while we were sightseeing. Laughing, I said, "We have to admire them for being enterprising entrepreneurs!"

The island of Rhodes belonged to Italy until 1948. Planning to spend his summers in Rhodes, Mussolini restored The Palace of Grand Master in the 1940s. Fate intervened, but his restoration included elaborate mosaic floors recycled from Byzantine churches and villas from early centuries.

In Lindos, we climbed to the top of the Acropolis, pausing to enjoy the panoramic views of the turquoise sea and St. Paul's Bay below the sheer cliffs. Massive stone columns defining the ancient Temple of Athena reach up to the sky. Closing my eyes, hand against a pillar that St. Paul and other disciples might have touched, I stood breathing in their soulful presence. Lagging behind, I delayed leaving to have a spiritual moment alone, and then ran ran to catch up with the others.

I read the guidebook while lounging on the deck as the Constellation sailed to Santorini. "Santorini was born from the wrath and anger of the volcano that guards the entrance of the island . . . and has been called 'The Devil's Island.' But when the volcano sleeps, its serene landscape has another nickname, 'The Paradise Island.'" Everyone crowded around the railing when white buildings perched on high cliffs came into view. Unconcerned about its violent history, we only saw a paradise.

"Look at the donkeys!" we shouted as we were ferried to the island in small boats. Scrambling out of the boats, the quaint sight of men holding the reigns of donkeys quickly turned into displeasure. We stood open-mouthed when one of the men said in broken English, "Donkeys take you up."

"We're not riding on donkeys!" Our other option—go back to the boat.

Waiting to get seated on a donkey taxi, I giggled as Mary B. rejected each donkey brought to her. "That one is too frisky. No, not that one, he has a mean look in his eye." Suddenly a man grabbed me, pushing me up on a donkey. Expecting Mary to mount first, I was unprepared, dismayed to be sitting askew on the donkey. Donkey had a mulish attitude and turned in the wrong direction, heading back to the donkey stalls. I worried I'd be trapped with the donkeys, a prisoner in their disgraceful quarters, while the others toured Santorini.

My donkey tender jerked the donkey around. Cursing, he slapped him into the right direction while I clung tightly to the reins, trying not to fall off as we trotted up the slippery path. Suddenly, my frisky donkey tried to pass Jan riding ahead of me. Her mule stubbornly refused to let us by. Each time my donkey tried to pass, her donkey would cut in front of him, swishing his dirty tail on me. Yuck! I tried to duck, but feared falling off if I leaned too far.

Mary B. still refused each donkey they brought. Losing patience, the donkey driver tossed her onto one despite her yelping. Her donkey decided to trot and she yelled, "Not so fast!" The donkey stopped short when the donkey man pulled its tail.

Clari's fast mount galloped past. My donkey tried to follow, but again Jan's jealous steed refused to let mine pass. Apparently they were enemies. Unable to stop laughing, I worried I'd fall off onto the white cobblestone steps thick with donkey dung.

The mile-long ascent ended just as I was beginning to get better acquainted with my new mule friend. At the top, we slid off our donkeys, cheering as late-comers arrived, flushed and disheveled, proud to have overcome their fear, but anxious to dismount.

Clari and I went off exploring and discovered a convent. A priest in white robes strolled into the little courtyard as we sneaked in to take a picture beside a huge pottery jar. Posing with us, he said that he was from Spain, but had studied theology in Washington D.C. He invited us into the beautiful little church and we said prayers for our safe return home.

Relieved to be transported down the mountain by Santorini's cable-car, we read in a brochure: "An interesting information: Here we must thank the "Nomikos Foundation," established in 1979 by shipowner Evangelos Nomikos, who gave all the expenses for the cable-car purchase . . ." We agreed that the tramway was "a charming travel" as we admired the view of dazzling blue water, white-washed buildings and round blue roofs. Jewels don't intrigue me, but I ached to take home one of the huge blue pottery jars. Aahhh, Santorini!

The sun descended in a magnificent pink sunset for our memorable last night on the Constellation. Wearing a white sundress I bought in Rhodes and sandals I bought in Santorini, I tripped off to "Greek Night." The waiters were dressed in black trousers, blue and white striped sweaters, wide red sashes, and wide smiles.

After our last gourmet dinner, the crew and staff presented a program of traditional Greek songs and dances. The cruise director taught us to yell "opa opa" for the best entertainment. "Opa opa", we yelled enthusiastically when a waiter picked up a table with his teeth. He danced without spilling the three bottles of beer on the table.

We left the islands yearning to stay longer. Years later, while walking through the Mall of America in Minneapolis, I stopped short when a painting of gleaming white buildings with bright blue doors shouted at me. Mykonos! The painting transported me back to a ship cruising Greek islands in the Aegean Sea exploring historical, picturesque islands.

An acrylic painting by my talented brother-in-law, Tom Karsnia, hangs in my kitchen, reminding me of the extraordinary Greek Islands: steps winding around tiers of white stucco houses with shiny blue shutters and doors.

Aahhh, Mykonos! Aahhh Santorini.

Chapter 13
April in Paris
Greece trip 1984, continued

Is this me, strutting down Champs-Élysée in a new fur coat?! Ignore dirty jeans and scuffed Adidas, I'm wearing mink. We flew from Greece to Charles de Gaulle Airport in Paris for an overnighter.

April in Paris is *C'est magnifique* no matter how brief! Our French tour director pointed out famous landmarks as we pressed our noses to the windows on our way to Hotel De France Et Choiseul.

Appearing unhappy that we cluttered up their elegant lobby with our stained luggage, the Hotel De France staff's disdainful coolness was a direct contrast to the warm welcome from the hotel in Portugal. Although, I admit we were a scruffy bunch, weary from lack of sleep, and shaky from close calls on the frightening bus trip from the airport. Several times, crazy drivers nearly crashed into our bus.

Clari and I gaped at the opulent furnishings in our room: an antique armoire, a silky-looking green loveseat and chair, and a marble-topped table strewn with Paris magazines. "What a contrast to that little gray shoebox aboard the ship!" Clari said. Silver accessories graced a white marble countertop on the old-fashioned sink in the white-tiled bathroom. We hung our fur coats in the fancy armoire while we bathed in the old-fashioned white tub with claw feet.

Strolling down the wide sidewalk lined with chestnut trees, I felt giddy. Afraid to step off the sidewalk with the mad French drivers speeding around the Arc de Triomphe. Napoleon built the Arc as a tribute to France's military glories; it was completed in 1836. Twelve avenues radiate around the Arc with cars roaring around it in all directions. We walked over to a parked cab. I asked, "Eiffel Tower?" The driver shook his head, "No Engleesh." Clari leaned over, pointing to her map, but jerked back quickly when he rolled up the window and shouted, "Walk."

Miffed from that snub, Clari suggested the Metropole. "Tony and I took it once, it's fast and clean." A man overheard us wondering how to find the subway station, and introducing himself as an American from Connecticut, he gave us directions.

Next, we battled with the turnstile in the station. Repeatedly, an iron bar stopped us. "My stomach must be black and blue from this bar," I moaned. A man in back of us growled, "Go get another ticket."

Clari and I stomped back to the ticket window. The ticket seller pantomimed, "Put ticket in, take ticket out." Back we trudged, tickets in hand. Sure enough, the machine spit the ticket out. Busy trying to barge through the turnstile, we hadn't noticed it pop up. Thankfully, our Connecticut friend was there to direct us to our train, waving off our thanks.

The glorious view of the Eiffel Tower in lights was worth the effort of getting there. However, kids were flying artificial birds or whizzing around on skateboards. Ducking from a flying bird zooming by, Clari said, "You'd think they'd have more respect for their famous landmark." The Eiffel Tower was built for Exposition Universelle in 1889, the tallest building in the world at that time. At first, Parisians hated it, but now it's the symbol of Paris.

We encountered no problems taking the Metro to join our group at The Lido for our 10:00 p.m. reservation. The curtains opened to beautiful girls in scanty costumes and vivid feathers high-kicking in perfect sync. Barb's husband, Jim, complained, "There was so much to see, I hardly got to look at the boobs." Illuminated by strobe lights, the Cabaret shows featured lively music and dancing, lovely scenery, and colorful costumes. The last scene opened with a replica of Rockefeller Center, St. Patrick's Cathedral visible in the background, and skaters on a real rink. Starting our trip with a visit to Rockefeller Center in New York, we're ending it with a New York grand finale at The Lido in Paris!

In the morning, sipping coffee in the dining room, we soaked up the sumptuous surroundings. Crystal chandeliers sparkled from a high ceiling. Our croissant was delicious and we lingered in the ambience, ignoring the snooty waiters ignoring us.

Catching glimpses of the gray-green River Seine from the bus, Clari whispered, "It's not as beautiful as our Rainy Lake." However, we have nothing like the impressive Pont Neuf Bridge, the oldest bridge crossing River Seine and built in the Roman style with huge concrete arches.

It's also the longest bridge in Paris, connecting the Ile de la Cite to the Louvre Museum. Paris was once a small village known as "Ile de la Cite" (City Island). Now, Paris has over two million people.

Our French guide warned, "Watch for pick pockets when we walk to the Louvre. They make their living by snatching purses." Sure enough, as we walked to the entrance of the Louvre, a pack of young Gypsy boys cruising for victims boldly swarmed around us like a cloud of gnats. They homed in on one of the older ladies, circling Margaret as easy prey. Our alert guide gave chase and they scattered, but we nervously held our purses tightly against our bodies.

The Louvre, built in the sixteenth century and once the home of French kings, now houses world treasures. The most famous painting of all, Mona Lisa, is in a room by herself. Peeking through a window because the room was closed that day, we thought Mona looked lonely. Another room held only Claude Monet paintings. As an owner of Claude Monet's paintings (reproductions), I thoroughly cherished seeing originals. Monet bought a large estate when he became wealthy, creating gardens to inspire his paintings until he died at age 86. Well, we have something in common—I create gardens too, but I rely on a digital camera for my pictures.

Like wild horses, we stampeded into HauteCoeur to buy reproductions of Louvre paintings after our speedy sampling of Louvre treasures. The salespeople were in a panic trying to wait on everyone galloping around the store. Apparently our shoppers didn't spend all their money in Greece!

Notre Dame Cathedral is magnificent! The French Gothic architecture with pointed arches and flying buttresses is impressive outside; inside, the cathedral holds nine thousand persons. The ancient part of the church, including the Pieta, was built when King Louis XIII reigned. The Blessed Mother holding Jesus looked at me soulfully as I reverently touched her hand. Notre Dame was built to inspire; over one hundred years later, it still inspires.

Latin floated over us as we tiptoed in the side aisles of the church during a Mass, gazing at chapels with art works from the seventeenth and eighteenth centuries. A few congregants were sitting in simple wooden chairs (I was surprised there were no pews with kneelers) scattered throughout the huge church. Our guide explained the stunning stained glass windows: "The south rose-window, looking like a bright star, depicts Christ in the New Testament. A blue window on the north is a symbol of night and of the Old Testament.

The guide said, "The Church Chancel was always built in the direction of the East so the priest can say Mass looking at the sun. People in the earlier centuries were afraid that every time the sun set, it might not come back; it would be the last day of living." How terrifying that would be, to worry that another day might not follow a sunset!

Rushing through this legendary church was frustrating, but we had a plane to catch. Stopping to light a candle on our way out, I caught up with the others before Bonnie realized I was missing. Thoughts of that glowing candle in Notre Dame Cathedral comforted me as we continued our journey.

Pouring rain soaked us as we staggered off the bus with our luggage at the airport. Damp but relieved, we settled into our seats on board the Boeing 747. Jim, wearing a bright yellow French beret, said, "Adieu, Paris. Have fun with our money!"

In New York, six of us thought we didn't have to worry about our luggage until Minneapolis and went through Customs with only our purchases and hand luggage. The official checking our declaration of purchases seemed impressed. "This is your entire luggage?" Yup. Proud of ourselves, Joan and I joined Sandy, Jan, Lillian and Corinne waiting outside Customs. I asked, "Where are the others?" Blankly, they shook their heads.

Running, searching through terminals, I returned to the same small group huddled together. Tears trickled down Corinne's cheeks, the other faces mirrored my panic. Seizing an opportunity to get back into Customs when several people came out, I heard a man shouting, "International Falls Tour!" My fear disappearing, I waved joyfully. "Here we are." The Customs official came storming over to us. "How did you get through Customs without your luggage? What did you think, Customs was going to deliver it to your bedroom in International Falls and unpack it for you?" *Oops.*

Hanging our heads, we meekly listened to his tongue lashing before going back to drag our big suitcases to the end of a long line. Afraid we'd miss our plane, Clari found the head of Customs to explain our problem. Apparently deciding we were dumb but honest, he escorted us through the line himself. Six naïve Minnesotans lost our aura of Parisian sophistication quickly.

We were grateful to get on the plane to Minneapolis. As you may recall from "Superlative Shopping Excursion" we plotted about presenting the coats to our husbands.

April in northern Minnesota brings the promise of spring coats to replace tired winter coats. My mink jacket went into storage immediately, waiting for winter. But November's bleak cloudy days were compounded by bleaker news. On November 4, 1984, the Insulite division of Boise Cascade Paper Mill closed its doors, terminating five hundred employees. Working in human resources, I met with the tragic-faced terminated workers. Unable to flaunt a new fur during that winter of depression, I mothballed the mink for a couple years.

Dove Island on Rainy Lake

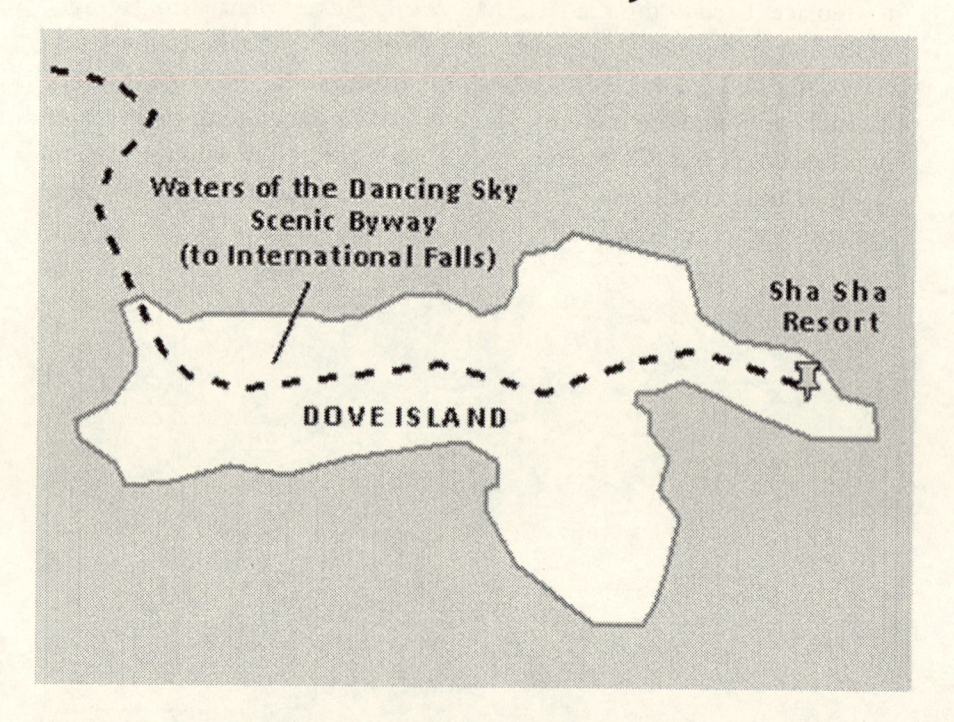

Chapter 14
The Birch Tree
Dove Island May 1990

Incredulously, Leo and I were building our dream house on Rainy Lake. I'd dreamed of a cabin on Rainy Lake every time I went fishing, first as a little girl with my dad, and then with my husband and kids. I'd written down this goal while teaching a pre-retirement class at Boise. It was in one of the lessons—that writing down goals helps make them happen. It worked!

With only a few weeks left before turning our house in town over to new owners, I drove the fourteen miles to Dove Island to check on the progress. Construction was not progressing. I grumbled to myself that apparently the light rain—barely a drizzle—kept the carpenters away.

Anxious to see the newly-constructed balcony upstairs, I crawled up the ladder in the open space for the stairs. Walking through the bedroom, I smiled at the Jacuzzi in the spacious bathroom, promising I'd soon enjoy its jets.

The balcony was larger than I'd expected, prompting a vision of morning coffee at a cute café table under the fragrant pine and golden birch trees. I'd have my own tree house with a bird's eye view! I cautiously crept across the cedar boards to peer down at the rocks below. A flicker of fear sent me scampering back to the door and safety.

The patio door had slammed shut behind me. My stomach churned as I stared at an open hole without a handle. Shoving, kicking, pounding—nothing opened the damned door. Poking my finger into the hole didn't release the latch. I was stuck outside in the rain and cold.

Yelling for the neighbors, both a distance away, brought no response. Of course, they wouldn't be outside on a cool rainy day in early May. But I yelled louder. "Joanne! Nellie!"

Another look at the menacing rocks below ruled out jumping. Convincing myself I could shimmy down the birch tree far enough to drop to the ground without breaking a leg, I carefully shuffled from the safety of the door. Reaching out my hand for a branch—I screamed. Slimy, slithering tent caterpillars covered the tree. Ugh! In Minnesota, the forest tent caterpillars show up every few years to devour the new leaves in the spring, leaving our forests stripped. They fall off the trees like raindrops, covering roads and sidewalks. I've learned to ignore the squishy worms under my feet when I'm walking, but I really hate it when they fall on my head. Now they're plopping down on the balcony with me.

Huddled in a fetal position, head on knees, I pondered my options: No jumping, no climbing down that slippery, wormy tree, no carpenters. A boat leaving Sha Sha Resort across the bay stirred the silence. Boats! I can flag down a boat. I stood up, but hunkered back down. I'd feel foolish. The fishermen would laugh.

Worms dropping onto the balcony, crawling toward me, forced me to jump up when I heard another motor. "HELP!" The boat sped away. I slumped back down, wet and shivering.

Another boat. "HELP!" It didn't stop. Moaning, I sank back down. But wait . . . my head jerked up. Did the boat stop? A voice floated up. "Is somebody yelling for help?"

I screamed, "Yes! Help! Come back!"

The boat turned around, stopped at our dock. "What do you want?"

"Get me off of here!" They tied up and—I couldn't believe my eyes—three women got out. One shouted, "Do we need a ladder?"

I yelled, "No! Come into the house, climb up the ladder, and open the door."

Three heads popped up from the ladder. Blinking away tears, I stumbled into the bedroom as soon as they opened the door. Shaky, but safe, I managed to laugh with them. "I feel so lucky that a boatload of women rescued me! Thank you!"

One said, "We live in Illinois and vacation here every year. Our friends will enjoy this fish story!"

"I came to check on the carpenters. We have to be out of our house by the end of June."

Looking around at the unfinished walls, worms swarming in through open windows, they said, "Good luck!"

Chapter 15
Loppet
Dove Island February 1993

My twelve-year-old grandson was hesitant about entering the Fun Ski in the Ski Loppet during Ice Box Days. International Falls celebrates its title, "Ice Box of the Nation," with three days of winter sports. When Adam hesitated, I coaxed, "We can go slow and quit when we want."

It was 20 degrees below zero the morning of the race. Adam's parents drove us to Voyageurs Park Visitors' Center to register and take our places with the other skiers. The stone park building reverberated with excited skiers clomping out to the start banner on Rainy Lake.

Skiers jockeyed for positions, eyeing the starter. Bang! The skiers were off! Some surged ahead at high speed, others spread out over the ice at a leisurely pace.

"Let's go, Grandma," Adam pleaded, impatient.

"We have to wait until all the racers are gone," I said.

Adam dug in his poles and shoved off as soon as the starter motioned us to go. The vast white expanse of ice gave no protection from a chilly wind swirling up snow. Ducking his face to protect his cold nose, Adam glided in tracks left by other skiers, with me behind him.

Catching up with some of the racers, Adam pushed harder, gliding further. As the route turned from north to west, the wind stopped battering his face and Adam picked up his pace, surprising me. Normally, I waited for him, now I was pushing to keep up with him.

Before skiing onto the Black Bay ski trail, Adam stopped to look at me. Grinning, I asked, "Do you want to keep going?"

"Yes!"

In the woods, the trail narrowed to a single track, and Adam maneuvered around skiers. Coming to a fork in the trail, Adam turned to the three-mile Ridge Trail with challenging hills. "Not that one, Adam. We stay on the one-mile for the Fun Ski."

Looking back at skiers he'd passed, Adam said, "I want to do the whole race." For a second, I thought about his parents expecting us back before long. Nah, he's with me and we're here with all these people, why would they worry? Grinning, I nodded and Adam slammed the sides of his skies into the hill, climbing up quickly.

Hot and sweaty after climbing hills, we drank thirstily when volunteers handed us cups of water. A yellow Skidoo stopped beside us and a rider wearing a big parka said "There you are, Adam. Your mother's waiting at the lodge, worried that you're lost."

"Hi, Tom, we're not lost. Adam decided we should join the race," I said.

Tom pulled a phone out of his jacket. "I'll call back to let them know you're safe." And he roared off.

Oops. I should have thought more about worried parents.

When we skied out of the woods, Sherry and Jim were waiting and hustled us into their Jeep. We weren't allowed to ski back to the finish line.

The next year, Adam and I skied through the finish line and won medals in our age groups.

Chapter 16
Patterns on the Mountain
Helena, Montana—July 1998

At a liturgy convention in Helena, Montana, the "Patterns on the Mountain" theme focused on changes in the church. In the evening, watching the changing patterns of the mountain from our room in the College of Montana dormitory where we were staying, Carol and I reflected on our own personal life changes.

Strangely, Carol and I had grown up across the alley from each other but didn't play together because she was younger. We raised our families on Ninth Street, but she lived on a different block. When, she and Jim moved to Dove Island we finally became friends.

(The Ninth Street neighbors on my block began a tradition of coffee and bran muffins every Saturday morning. I met Norma Krats, Bernice Corrin, Helen Nilson, and Helen Matson in the alley for the three-block walk to Bridgeman's. We've maintained that tradition for over forty years, although some of the faces are gone, others added, and now I drive in from the lake.)

Patterns are continually changing. My personal change was retirement after thirty-five years of rushing to work every morning. A leisurely summer (after a thorough spring housecleaning) sitting on the deck capturing hummingbirds or Rainy Lake scenes with my camera led to creating a small business, KarsCards, with the photos.

Retirement led to five-mile walks with Carol on the historic road, Waters of the Dancing Sky on Highway 11 leading to Voyageurs National Park. (VNP commemorates the voyageurs, French-Canadian fur traders who traveled Rainy Lake, starting in the mid 1600s. Rainy Lake is sixty miles long with nine hundred twenty-nine miles of shoreline)

Walking and talking led to Carol's convincing me to become a member of St. Thomas Aquinas Church's Worship Commission. I was ready for schedules again and threw myself into volunteering. After driving thirteen miles, when I reached the edge of town I had to convince my Buick we weren't going to the paper mill. But first, I had to remember which meeting I was attending. Retirement is not for the faint-hearted!

Reviewing my past life journey challenged me to think about my future life journey, giving me the impetus to enroll in writing classes at Rainy River Community College. I became addicted to writing. Becoming a "college girl" helped dilute thoughts of "being old."

After the Montana conference, six of us rented a van, giving us another liturgical experience as we observed the park's recovery from the devastating fire in 1988, exclaiming in awe at God's re-creation of the spectacular beauty of the park. And that's how I had the chance to visit an awesome conference and another awesome national park!

YELLOWSTONE NATIONAL PARK JULY 1998

The spectacular beauty of the park
Unfolds as we peer from the windows of the car.
We disembark to exclaim in awe at the grandeur of it all:
Sizzling springs in desolate spots
With signs warning us—they are scalding hot.
Bubbling mud pots invite visions
Of wicked witches mixing potions.
Steaming, gurgling geysers and mud
Bubble up visions of hell to come.
Old Faithful teasing with small spurts of spray
Before exploding in a vivacious display.
At Artist's Point we gasp at the view
Of vivid lava rock gorges He has hewn
Using minerals and water as tools.
Thundering waterfalls crashing down
Canyon walls carved deeper now
By the force of the mighty cascade
Ceaselessly blasting rock away.
A raging blaze left lonely lodgepole pines naked,
Satans's fury destroyed forest sacred.
Tiny trees flourish—a new generation
Defies the fiery hills' destruction.
We exclaim in awe at God's re-creation.

Chapter 17
Ageless Magic
Disneyland—February 1999

I waited a long time before getting my trip to Disneyland. My four-year-old grandson and I flew off on a magic carpet to Florida for our first Disney Pilgrimage in 1999. I felt like Alice in Wonderland stepping into pages of fairy tales. We stood spellbound by the view of Cinderella's Castle towering over an elaborate Victorian town in the Magic Kingdom.

Tyler's parents, Jayne and Nathan, and my husband, Grandpa Leo, were prepared with maps, guide books, and directions from friends. The obligatory autograph book was tucked safely away in Jayne's purse, ready for the Disney characters. Collecting autographs and photos is important while visiting Disneyland! Tyler and I, carefree, skipped into the land of magic.

"Early morning is the best time to start filling up that autograph book," Jayne said. In Toontown Hall of Fame, Disney characters cheerfully pose for pictures. Tweedle Dee and Dum were the first to sign Tyler's book, playfully writing their names upside down. Minnie posed with moms and kids, looking as adorable in her polka dots as I remembered her from my youth. Mickey was charming in a tuxedo. When I heard Goofy's infectious laugh, I couldn't resist running up to get my picture taken with him.

Long, long ago when I was a child, there were only a few Disney characters—Minnie and Mickey Mouse, Donald Duck, Pluto and Goofy. We didn't know them as intimately as children do now. Movies were rare occasions; neither TV nor videos had been invented. Our radios and phonographs that played large records were the latest technology. I became acquainted with Winnie the Pooh and a few new characters watching TV with my kids. As we left Toontown, Tyler told me, "I like Pluto and Eeyore best! But I like Tigger and Winnie the Pooh too." So many choices!

Grandpa Leo was elected to accompany Tyler on the scary rides. Seeing how easily I got scared, Tyler warned, "Peter Pan's Flight will take us flying right into Peter Pan's fight with Captain Hook and the bad guys." The bloody fight was scary, and we calmed down on the boat ride among a lovely exhibit of dolls, singing along to *It's a Small World*.

Cinderella's Fairy Godmother greeted us when we arrived at the castle for lunch, tired and hungry after our adventures. A Medieval waiter at Cinderella's Royal Table crowned Tyler a young prince; Jayne and I were addressed as "My Lady," Nathan and Grandpa Leo as Lords. Waitresses wore lovely medieval dresses with lace and ruffles, but Tyler snickered at the knickers the waiters wore. The butter, molded into statues of Mickey, was a clue to the all-pervasive motif at Disney.

The Monorail's tracks sped soundlessly on concrete bridges over Disney World, stopping on top of the Contemporary Hotel. We walked down to Chef Mickey-Minnie Café, Tyler's favorite place to eat. Hosts Minnie and Mickey, Pluto and Goofy, Chip and Dale greeted guests wearing tall, white chef hats. At the Celebration of Mickey kids, and adults acting like kids, noisily waved green cloth napkins while the characters danced and sang,

An hour ahead of an afternoon parade at MGM, we settled Tyler on a curb. Mulan the beautiful Chinese girl who saved her country, is honored with rich Chinese ceremony and waved to the crowd from a huge float, accompanied by an army of warriors in red brocade.

It felt good to sit in a movie theater watching Ariel get her legs and her prince in *Voyage of the Little Mermaid*. Tyler said, "I didn't like that bad Ursula, but she made that little mermaid into a girl so she could walk and love."

Early one morning we set off for the Kilimanjaro Safari to Animal Kingdom, following the beat of drums to the African village Harambe. (An African safari is on my bucket list, but I suspect this will have to do.) Tyler enjoyed bouncing up and down over muddy roads overflowing with water as we wound through the jungle in open-air trucks. At lunch Tyler chattered about seeing lions and tigers, elephants and gorillas.

The Tree of Life in Animal Kingdom is a tall, fifty foot-wide artificial tree carved with animals in the roots, trunk, and branches. Tyler explained: "Whoever gets dead gets put on the tree and then painted in. God sent them to be on the tree." Inside the Tree, Flik and Hopper host *It's Tough to Be a Bug*. The bugs retaliate against the audience for the way humans treat bugs, threatening us with giant fly swatters and bug sprays. Afterward, I asked Tyler if he got scared when bugs buzzed and flew out of the screen to spit at us. Tyler replied, "Grandma, it's just pretend. If you take off the funny glasses (3-D glasses), they go away."

At The Haunted Mansion, howling wolves, bats, and cobwebs didn't scare Tyler, but he buried his head when the witch cackled and beckoned with her bony finger. I chuckled at his comment about the skeletons: "I didn't like those guys skinned down to their bones."

Splash Mountain in Frontierland's Old West, bragged about boats going forty miles per hour down the fifty-two foot drop at Splash Mountain, advertising it as a screamer. I screamed! Grandpa Leo bravely rode the boat several times; he and Tyler were frequent passengers on the boat ride in Snoopyville at Mall of America in Minneapolis. I cruised the shops.

At the Universe of Energy, Bill Nye, the science guy, and his companion, Ellen Degeneres, smashed through the jungle running from the huge dinosaurs. Tyler, an expert on dinosaurs who loves his stuffed dinosaur collection, told me the names of all the screaming dinosaurs that roamed the earth billions of years ago. Tyler giggled when Ellen told a snake, "You have a bad attitude."

We were sprinkled with magic even before landing in Disneyland. Our son in Houston and our nephew in Portland were simultaneously scheduled for conferences in Orlando. We were overjoyed that they'd arrive on February 9th, Leo's sixty-fifth birthday. Allen and Andy came with a cake to celebrate Leo's milestone birthday, a magical finale to Disneyland!

Before the plane landed back in Minneapolis, Tyler said, "I hope it's summer here, too." It wasn't. But Tyler adapted back to his real world. I'm amazed at the amount of information processed by a pre-schooler, at how many characters and plots my young grandson retained. This dreamlike journey into imagination sometimes assaulted my senses, but Tyler sped in and out of fantasy and reality with ease.

Ireland

Chapter 18
Searching Dublin for a Cousin
Ireland September 1998

Faith in the luck of the Irish and the help of Leprechauns disguised as live Irish angels made a trip to Ireland an unforgettable journey for four women who left Minnesota hoping to find a cousin with an unknown address and unlisted phone number.

Mary Beth Foyt, a flight attendant for Continental Airlines, invited her mother, Leo's sister, Peggy Foyt, to fly with her to Ireland in September, 1998. I'd started writing *A Bit of Irish Gold* about Leo's family history and longed to research their Irish genealogy. When Peggy told me about the trip, I immediately ran to the phone and dialed Rosie Rasmussen, another sister-in-law, "Peggy and Mary Beth are going to Ireland. Let's go with them!"

Promising our families we would not go into Northern Ireland because thirty Catholics had recently been killed by a bomb in Omagh, we flew to Dublin.

We ran after long-legged Mary in the Dublin Airport, dragging our luggage, weak from lack of sleep. Well, maybe we'd enjoyed first class a wee bit too much. Mary Beth and her mother had gallantly surrendered their first class seats to Rosie and me. How could we refuse that good-looking male attendant who insisted on refilling our wine glasses?

We chanted as Mary drove the rental car on the left side of the road, "Left—left— left— Mary Beth." When she forgot, menacing buses and lorries threatened to smash us, making us duck as they headed directly at us. Mary swerved just in time, giggling as she switched lanes, "I have trouble telling left from right!" We noticed!

Our guardian angels rode shotgun as we maneuvered a maze of narrow lanes until we found the little seaport of Howth. We tumbled out of the car, grateful to be alive, at our reserved bed and breakfast.

Innkeeper Sean welcomed us cordially, serving tea in the living room. Talkative Sean was torn between preparing our rooms and talking. Clutching sheets to his chest, he paused to join our conversation; wearily, we wished he'd stop chattering and put the sheets on our beds. The B&B had small rooms, narrow twin beds, a tiny bath, and even tinier showers with just a wee bit of water flow.

We decided Sean was a kind Leprechaun thinly disguised as innkeeper. Sean overheard us discussing how to find our long-lost cousin, Michael Sullivan. My daughter Jayne met Michael while she was in Ireland, but her last letter to him had come back stamped "Address Unknown." Sean actively took over the search. He called his sister, who worked at a school close to Michael's old address in Coolock, to get directions. He mapped the route for us, giving more directions as he waved us off in the morning. "You cannot leave Dublin until you find your cousin," he yelled as we backed out of the driveway.

Pedestrians jumped when Mary drove up the curb while Peggy yelled out the window for directions; luckily we found the house before having an accident. Pounding on the door before peeking through the picture window, I called, "Come look! This house is lovely." Undaunted that nobody was home, I scribbled a note with our names and Sean's phone number. "We can call Sean to see if Michael contacted him," Peggy noticed a man across the street unloading tomatoes from the trunk of his car. She ran over to ask, "Does Michael Sullivan live there?"

"Michael? The bloke moved away over a year ago."

"Oh, no!" we wailed.

With sad faces, the four of us straggled across the street to stare at the bearer of bad news. Michael's former neighbor said, "Come in. I'll make tea." Without a second thought, we dejectedly followed him into his house.

In his tiny kitchen he shook our hands, introducing himself as Thomas. "I'm a retired military man," he said, his short-cropped steel-gray hair and regal bearing proclaiming his military past.

With glum faces, we sat around the kitchen table. Thomas pulled out the phone book. "I'll try to locate Michael." He called Michael's house, Michael's mobile phone, Michael's parish rectory, and the school where Michael's wife teaches. His patient persistence finally resulted in a call back from Michael's wife, Betty. Betty insisted, "He should be home, he's painting the house." But Michael did not answer.

Over steaming mugs of tea, Thomas confided that a man with criminal connections, a drug dealer, now owned Michael's house.

"There used to be lots of break-ins and burglaries in this neighborhood, but not anymore. He took care of that."

Mary Beth jumped out of her chair. "A drug dealer!"

Wide-eyed, Peggy whispered, "It must have been angels who intervened so the drug dealer wasn't home."

I said, "Well, I hope the angels are still with us because I put a note in the mail box with our names and where we're staying." We debated about retrieving it. "What if somebody comes home when I have my hand in the mailbox?" Shoving worries aside that the drug dealer would track us down, we reassured ourselves, "Our Leprechaun Sean will take care of us."

Thomas dialed Michael again, and when Michael answered on the second ring, he said, "I'm entertaining four women who want to see you." All of us agreed 'twas an angel who pulled Michael into the house for a spot of tea. Michael rang the doorbell before we'd completed a tour of Thomas's back yard wine cellar and still. Rosie had already sampled his homemade Irish Poteen (Irish Illegal Spirits) and accepted a bottle to share with the other four sisters at our annual sisters' reunion.

Sure, and was it not the luck of the Irish that Michael was on holidays the exact days we would be there? Doubly lucky because he's a social worker and is taking college classes. Despite his normally hectic schedule, painting his house was put on hold while he acted as our chauffeur, guide, historian, and chef. Michael gave us a quick introduction to Dublin while driving us to his house. Phoning Betty he said: "I'm surrounded by a gaggle of Americans. They're a mad lot and I'm bringing them home."

Ignoring our promises not to go to Northern Ireland, we squeezed into Michael's car for a trip to Dungannon, vowing to keep our trip north a secret until we returned home. It made us nervous when we were stopped at the northern border by garda with rifles, but Michael had made the trip hundreds of times and they recognized him.

Our eyes filled with tears when Michael showed us important family places in Dungannon: the church where the Karsnia grandparents, Matt and Annie Donahue, were married, the store where Matt met Annie on his way to America. We toured cemeteries filled with ancestors. Our visit to a cathedral in Armagh became a chapter in my book, *A Bit of Irish Gold*. What better research? Michael said: "T'was the year 432 when St. Patrick sailed to Armagh and this cathedral honors him." He showed us a room with hats of Cardinals dangling from the ceiling. "When a Cardinal's soul goes to heaven, his hat falls down."

Our last evening in Ireland we tapped our feet to Irish music in a pub in Malahide where Betty's cousin played guitar in the four-man band. Everybody in the pub treated us as celebrities! The musicians joined us at our table, making us feel even more important. Betty said, "They don't get paid, they love to play so much they just show up at pubs."

Michael added, "They are a brilliant bunch!" "Brilliant "is one of Michael's favorite words—and we think he is absolutely brilliant!

Saying good-bye the next morning, Michael expressed his wonder at our luck at finding him: "There is serendipity in the human condition which surpasses logic and reason."

Four women agreed. Our search would have been futile relying on logic and reason instead of faith—faith in angels, leprechauns, and Irish luck.

Chapter 19
London's Hop on, Hop Off
2001

My second trip to Ireland, with my husband and daughter, was to fulfill a pact that Jayne and her dad made eighteen years ago. When she came home after three months in Ireland with a St. Scholastica College study group, she was determined to return. While there, the students lived in thatch-roofed stone cottages in Louisburgh, a rural town on the windy western coast. They filled baskets with peat for the fireplace and scheduled showers because the trickle of hot water disappeared quickly. Sheep sauntered down Main Street and the postman delivered mail by bicycle. Despite the primitive conditions, Jayne fell in love with the Irish people, including her father's relatives. "Dad, you even look like them!"

The return to Ireland was delayed as Jayne followed the cycles of young adult life: college graduation, jobs, studying for a Masters' degree, marriage, and a child. Jayne seized the occasion of a business trip to London in 2001 as an opportune time, quickly organizing this long-dreamed-about Irish journey.

Then the media broadcast news about a crisis in England caused by foot and mouth disease (FMD). Hearing every day about the devastation causing thousands of people and animals to die, we decided to cancel the trip. We called Leo's cousin Michael, our Irish relative who had been overjoyed to drop his paintbrush to show four Karsnia women a "brilliant time." Michael said, "Cancel the trip? What's the problem? Life goes on as normal." Still scared, we accepted Michael's word that it wasn't a problem and bravely flew off to London.

Staying at the (pricey) Thistle Tower prompted us to spend our first hours at the near-by London Tower, an incredible edifice begun in the reign of William the Conqueror (1066-1087). Yeoman Warders dressed in traditional medieval costumes of the fourteenth century still guard the Tower, doubling as guides. Our witty guide entertained as well as informed us about this early site of London history that had served as a residence for kings, served as a fortress, and served as a prison. Several rooms displayed an amazing armory of spears, blunderbusses, pistols, cannons, armor for horses, armor for riders and foot soldiers.

The Bloody Tower had seen many assassinations. Two of Henry VIII's six wives were beheaded there—Anne Boleyn and Catherine Howard. Thousands of hangings were viewed from the nearby Hung, Drawn, and Quartered Pub.

Touring London on the Hop on and Hop off bus while Jayne attended meetings, Leo and I visited London landmarks. When we arrived at Buckingham Palace for Changing of the Guard, we expected only a dribble of people because Prime Minister Tony Blair had complained that morning on TV that foot and mouth disease was needlessly affecting tourism in the U.K, criticizing the media for over-reacting. From what Blair said, devastation from the loss of tourism was more of a crisis than the devastation caused by FMD.

But there were solid crowds in front of the gate at the palace. An overflow of tourists stood across at Hyde Park and many were piled on Queen Victoria's statue. A golden winged angel on top of Queen Victoria, arms stretching up, seemed to be imploring for help from the heavens.

Police in lime green slickers guarded the roped-off square. The marching band wearing long gray coats cinched with white belts, gold helmets glittering, led the Horse Guards clip-clopping through the mall, their full black or red coats enveloping both man and beast. There are five different regiments of footguards; the plumes in their helmets denote which regiment they are from. Guarding the palace is a small part of their duty; the other, as front-line infantrymen in war, is far more demanding.

Picking up Jayne at Thistle Towers, we boarded another bus. The new narrator focused on different sights and information, so the second time around was as interesting as the first, plus we hopped off for a loud rock and roll lunch at Hard Rock Café.

At the end of the tour, the gray-haired driver stood at the door asking passengers if they knew how to get to their destinations, saying, "We don't like to lose passengers." The tour ended at Picadilly Circus, which is the theater district, and we expected for find Cambridge Theater easily, but his concern touched me. However, we got lost in the maze of streets and a kind pedestrian led us to the theater.

The Beautiful Game, a musical by Ben Elton and Andrew Lloyd Webber, was a perfect segue as we learned more about Ireland's "Terrible Trouble." Chris Tarrant of Capital Radio wrote an excellent headline for the play: "Andrew Lloyd Webber and Ben Elton's absolutely stunning, incredibly funny, brilliant, romantic musical."

The story takes place in Belfast as the sixties draw to a close. High-school boys want to be left alone to play football, and life is just beginning for Mary and John, who are taking their first tentative steps towards a love destined to last a lifetime. But during the Terrible Trouble in Northern Ireland, violence escalates and their lives are disrupted.

Our relatives in Ireland lived through "The Terrible Trouble." Jayne and I had heard Michael's stories on our previous visits. Danny, his younger brother beaten by Protestants, is still suffering from the aftereffects of having his head pounded on the sidewalk. Driving from Dublin to Dungannon in Northern Ireland to visit his mother, sister and brother, Michael drove past garda with rifles for many years.

Leaving the Cambridge Theatre we encountered a crush of people and our own "trouble." London theatre is impressive, but the congested streets afterward are horrible. London cabs are colorful and plentiful at noon, but painfully lacking in the black of midnight. Taking the subway is a quick and inexpensive way to travel, and at the first subway sign, we ran down the steps and arrived safely back at luxurious Thistle Towers.

Exhausted from our busy day, I tumbled into bed, anxious to get rested up for our trip to Dublin in the morning. Jayne was excited to see Michael again after an eighteen-year absence, Leo was eager to meet his cousin for the first time, and I knew that Michael would show us a "brilliant" time.

Chapter 20
Ireland's Terrible Trouble
2001 continued

Early in the morning, reluctantly leaving our luxurious room at Thistle Towers but gulping at the bill, we caught a cab to London's airport and joined the crowd at RyanAir terminal. The no-frills airline doesn't reserve seats, we stood poised with the other passengers to race from the terminal to the plane. Jostling our way to the front, we outran the pack and found seats together.

Michael and Betty picked us up at the airport. Michael, our excellent and knowledgeable guide, immediately donned his guide persona.

First stop, Trinity College, where only Protestants had been allowed to attend since it was founded by Queen Elizabeth in 1592, Michael proudly said he was one of the first Catholics students. We looked in wonder at the fabulous Book of Kells, magnificent manuscripts painstakingly illustrated by Irish monks in the fifth century. The Book of Kells with its swirling calligraphy is considered Ireland's national treasure. Two of the four illustrated Gospels, created in monasteries from sixth to ninth centuries are on display in Trinity at one time.

In the spectacular Long Library, which is two hundred ten feet long and lined with marble busts of scholars, Michael said he'd climbed the high ladders to retrieve books from the two hundred thousand antique books and manuscripts stored from floor to the second story.

On Sunday, Michael drove us into Northern Ireland in his black Ford. "Henry Ford was one of our own." (Henry Ford was born in Michigan, but his father was born in County Cork, Ireland. The Irish are proud of the Irish!) Michael's brother, Danny, met us in Dungannon Square. In the church where Leo's grandparents, Matt and Annie Donahue were married in 1910, we stood reverently in front of the Station of the Cross dedicated to Annie's parents. On Perry Street, Leo posed in front of the shop Annie's family once owned, now boarded up from bombings in the 1970s. In the cemetery, Michael introduced us to family tombstones.

On our way to and from Dungannon in County Tyrone, we drove through County Cooley where the only incident of foot and mouth disease had been found. "We almost cancelled our trip because of the media," I exclaimed. At garda checkpoints, we drove over disinfectant mats, and on our way back to Dublin the garda sprayed Michael's car with disinfectant. Disinfectant mats were placed at the doorway of every establishment throughout Ireland, we walked over them automatically. Michael said, "Irish people are a wee bit critical of England for not taking more precautions."

Monday morning, Jayne slid behind the wheel of a rental Toyota, excited about driving to St.Scholastica Study Center in Louisburgh. Michael told Jayne it would take about twenty minutes to become acclimated to driving on the left side of the road, but she turned into A.J. Foyt in less than ten minutes.

Driving across the middle of Ireland from the east coast of Dublin to Louisburgh in the west, motorways with four lanes decreased to "N" roads. I thought N stood for narrow but it meant National roads. National highways in Ireland are narrow lanes dominated by threatening lorries and buses demanding the entire road. Stone fences and wild hedges sprawling into the road squeeze them even narrower—and watch out for "dangerous bends!"

Ireland's city streets are a labyrinth of cars parked on the sidewalk or in the middle of the road, wherever it's convenient for the driver to depart. Cows also have the right of way on N highways as they amble from one pasture to one greener on the other side.

Turning a corner, Jayne screeched to a halt as a flock of fluffy sheep filled the highway. We followed behind Irish sheep in our rented Japanese car, drinking in the pastoral scene: A red-headed boy about ten years old, clad in a blue rain slicker, strode down the middle of the road in red boots matching his hair, waving a stick with authority behind the sheep. Enchanted by the grin circling his face, I fell in love with him as I snapped a photo. The boy's father drove ahead in a modern van, shepherding his sheep to the next pasture. Watching the sheep follow each other through an open gate in the stone fence, I knew I'd never forget our favorite traffic jam.

In County Clare, Atlantic Ocean waves were smashing against rocks as we drove on the Burren coastal road past porous gray rock and barren limestone. Plants cling to life in nooks and crannies, and we were clinging to life as Jayne drove at breakneck speed to get us to Bunratty for our medieval banquet reservation. Thankfully, we arrived at the banquet alive and on time.

At the incredible Cliffs of Moher towering six hundred fifty feet high for a five-mile stretch, wild waves crashed to the top of the huge rocks, competing with the thunder during a vicious storm. Spellbound, we ignored the wind whipping us as we watched nature's noisy fury.

Our last day on the road, we drove into the port city of Waterford and the famous factory founded in 1783 by two brothers. Exquisite chandeliers in the lobby, exquisite crystal on display, and exquisite works of art created by master blowers persuaded us to buy Waterford vases.

Every New Year's Eve, as the Waterford ball drops in New York City, I remember my visit to the factory, watching talented artists forming glass treasures.

Chapter 21
Excitement at Gate 38
2001 continued

Returning to London after our brilliant Ireland visit, we wearily waited in Gatwick Airport at gate 38 for our plane to Minneapolis. Repeated warnings over the loud speaker grated on our nerves: "Do not leave your bags unattended. Bags unattended will be destroyed." Too exhausted to move after traveling around the Emerald Island, we were not about to leave our bags. The three of us sprawled in the lounge alternately reliving fabulous memories of our trip, but yearning to be home.

We'd visited castles and cathedrals, fortresses and whitewashed thatched cottages; we were well-acquainted with stone walls and thick hedges scraping at our car. We'd joined Lords and Ladies drinking mead at a medieval banquet in Bunratty Castle, and learned to appreciate the art of drinking Guinness in rural pubs. We'd prayed in the shrine at Knock and gazed at many monastic sites scattered across the island. We'd listened to the lilting Irish language and lively Irish music. We'd captured a Leprechaun in Connemara. Jayne's six-year-old son had asked before she left, "Are you going to Ireland to catch a leprechaun?" Finnegan, a soft leprechaun playing a concertina and wearing a happy grin under his green hat, was a perfect gift for Tyler.

Fabulous landscapes fascinated us at every turn, from mountains down to rocky shore. Short walls of rock staggered up mountains, crisscrossing fields of green; we marveled at the hard labor it took to build those walls. Old stone structures, constructed from the land, are now being reclaimed by the land. Crumbling stone cottages look like giant flower pots, tall trees forming new roofs.

Giggling, I reminded Jayne, "Michael told you, 'let the people behind worry about passing you.'"

Leo laughed, "It was the people ahead of you who had to worry. There was only one car on the road that you didn't pass."

Leo, on his first visit to the land his grandparents emigrated from, felt he'd returned to his homeland. Jayne's long-delayed poignant pilgrimage renewed old friendships. My second trip was a nostalgic return to renew friendships with "The Relatives," revisit Dublin and Dungannon, and discover new wonders in Ireland.

Another announcement seeped through our mummified brains. "Will the person who left luggage unattended at Gate 38 in front of the game machine please return." I jerked up at the third announcement, feeling a jolt of fear. A few feet away, two security police stood over a green duffel bag. As the announcements continued, Jayne and I wordlessly moved further away from the suspect baggage. It was a relief to get away from the annoying announcement when we boarded the plane.

Leo was tugged awake from a nap when a woman grabbed his foot. Crawling in the aisle, she'd been searching under the seats. Apologizing, she started searching the overhead bins, shooting questions at her son, a sleepy dark-haired boy about seven years old. Intuitively I asked, "Are you looking for a backpack?" Looking at me hopefully, she nodded.

"There was a green backpack lying on the floor at the airport by gate 38. They announced it over and over." She began a mother's tirade, but soon I saw the sobbing boy getting comforted on his mother's lap. Oddly, I felt comforted too, and relieved that we were returning home safely from a trip to the past that united us with relatives for the future.

Chapter 22
Serching for Skeletons
March 2006

What magic lures visitors to Ireland? What mysticism makes them ignore the rain and blustery winds and narrow roads to traipse through ruins and medieval castles? Is it the warmth of the Irish people? Is it the beauty of the green? Is it to partake of the spirits in the limitless Irish pubs?

Bonding with Ireland isn't only for full-blooded Irish. Leo ignores his Polish ancestry. Jayne, after visiting Ireland as a college student, returned full-blooded Irish, ignoring her Polish, French and German heritage. Our twelve-year-old grandson Tyler, with only one-eighth Irish blood, instantly became an Irish lad when he put on a green Ireland sweatshirt. I'm only Irish by marriage, but when Jayne invited Leo and me to go to Ireland with her and Tyler, I was raring to go on a third trip.

Tyler, with a red backpack and wearing his white Abercrombie hat backwards, ran to hug Leo and me when he saw us waiting by Chile's in the Minneapolis airport. Grateful that the plane was only half full when it promptly taxied off for our four-thousand-mile flight to London, we each stretched out over two seats. A wet washcloth woke me up shortly after I'd finally drifted to sleep. I would have preferred sleeping instead of eating a breakfast of yogurt, fruit sauce and an inedible biscuit.

Deplaning in London at 3:30 a.m. we jammed our luggage into a mini-car while the taxi driver leisurely read his paper. By the time we checked in at Hyde Park Hotel, we were anxious to tour London and bought tickets from the concierge for The Big Bus.

Tyler's favorite hop-off place was the Tower of London, an incredible structure begun during the English reign of William the Conqueror (1066-1087). Yeoman Warders guarding the Tower, retired military who are required to take years of classes to qualify for the job, are dressed in traditional medieval costumes of the fourteenth century.

Listening intently to his ear phones about prisoners that were tortured, murdered, beheaded and hung, Tyler kept disappearing into corners searching for skeletons. I chuckled as I recalled his comment about skeletons in The Haunted House at Disneyland: "I didn't like those guys skinned down to their bones." What a difference eight years can make!

Sir Walter Raleigh was one of the most famous prisoners. Jane Grey was queen for nine days before Mary of Scotland had her beheaded. In medieval days they had no qualms about torturing. A clergyman escaped to tell about having nails pounded into his hands in preparation for his hanging.

A brief video of Queen Elizabeth on her Coronation Day wearing bejeweled robes and crowns primed us for the Crown Jewels. We rode around the dazzling display on a moving sidewalk. Even Tyler was amazed at the jeweled crowns, scepters and swords, the gold altar plates and other church accessories enclosed in glass cases. A massive wine goblet that could serve thousands seemed like the final outrage when so many people are starving, reminding me of our revulsion at the Sistine Chapel's excess.

Walking past the gate built over the Thames River where prisoners were brought in by ship, signage identified "The Murder Hole" and "Torture at the Tower." A tree next to the Marble Arch served as a gallows that could hang twenty-four people at one time. Supposedly, one hundred thousand people attended the hanging of the famous burglar, Jack Shepard; spectators poured into The Hung, Drawn and Quartered Pub for the best view.

London has had disasters as bad, or worse, than our modern catastrophes. Barely recovered from a major plague causing the death of over one hundred thousand Londoners, the great London Fire in 1666 destroyed over three-fourths of the city, making another one hundred thousand people homeless. The great architect, Christopher Wren, designed fifty-one churches after the fire.

After two days of touring in London, while having a snack at the London airport before boarding the plane to Dublin, Jayne said, "You need a lesson in eating 'the Irish Way.' Michael insisted I eat the 'proper way' when I visited him twenty-three years ago. Keep your knife in the right hand and the fork in the left; you never put down either utensil." I didn't adapt well, but Tyler perfected it.

Chapter 23
Irish Wonders
2006 continued

Disembarking from RyanAir in the Dublin airport, we spied Michael leaning against a round column wiggling his fingers at us. Driving us to his house, he updated us on the economy. "The good news is the economy in Ireland has improved, the endless poverty ended. The caveat—prosperity changed the landscape. Cranes dot towns and villages, rows of identical houses creep over the hills, and toll ways are being constructed. For the first time in history, immigration into Ireland exceeded emigration out. Not only are the young Irish moving back, making Ireland the nation with the youngest population, but other nationalities as well." Michael added regretfully, "The purity of the Irish population will soon be diluted."

Michael served another of his famous meals along with information: roast chicken, garlic mashed potatoes, and mushy peas. (We rave about mushy peas on every trip—I've never tasted them anywhere else—yum! Betty said they have to be steeped the night before.)

"Right now, it's the most peace they've ever had in Ireland. You can go into Northern Ireland without problems. They no longer have armed guards at checkpoints. I don't think Americans realize the role that former President Clinton played in bringing peace to Ireland, but the Irish give Clinton the credit. Clinton was on the phone negotiating for forty-eight hours. Without him it would not have happened."

At our B&B in the morning we enjoyed a typical Irish breakfast: a perfectly fried egg, two sausages, two slices of thick bacon, soda bread, white toast, orange juice, coffee, and tea. We greeted three women at another table who said they were teachers from Maryland. Laughing, one said, "We're waiting for Carol; she runs in marathons, but she's a little slow today. We went on a tour of Jamesons, and instead of finishing our tour in a gift shop, we stopped in the bar with free whiskey."

As Jayne maneuvered the car out of the tight parking spot to drive to Louisburg, all four women gathered around giving directions. Listening to Irish music, we set off for the study center Jayne had attended eighteen years ago, following a "dual carriageway" until a sign warned "End of dual carriageway NOW." Now meant we were back to narrow roads with sheep and cattle roaming the rolling green.

In County Mayo, we again admired the stone fences criss-crossing fields and trees growing out of roofless stone houses sinking back into the earth. As we got closer to Louisburg, Jayne pointed to Crough Patrick Mountain. "When I was at St. Scholastica Study Center, on a beautiful sunny day we talked our teachers into letting us climb the mountain instead of sitting in the classroom." Today, nobody asked to go mountain climbing.

Jayne said, "When we were here five years ago we didn't see the expensive cars like these BMW's and Audi's on the road." Driving into the St. Scholastica Study Center, she cried, "Oh, no! The thatch roof is gone!" Five years ago, she was thrilled that cottage number 5, where she had lived as a college girl, still had a thatch roof. A girl in the doorway of the cottage watched as we stopped in the driveway, and Jayne boldly asked if we could go in. She brought us in, introducing us to her roommate sitting at the kitchen table.

Jayne told them she had lived in the cottage twenty-three years ago. "We had to heat with peat. In the morning, we took turns getting up a half hour early to turn on the hot water for showers. Only two people could take a two-minute shower, so the four of us alternated showers." Pointing at the washing machine, she said, "We hitch-hiked to Westport to do our laundry." Their facial expressions revealed that they preferred their more modern living conditions.

In the car, Jayne said, "I liked it the way it was when I went there. Remember how bummed I got when we came back to the states? We formed a support group because we missed Ireland so much. But now, it's changed."

In a Louisburg pub, a crackling fire in the fireplace warming us, Leo and I admired the bartender's skill at drawing a pint of Guinness. The bartender said, "It's an art," as he drew pints for us. "You have to draw slowly, let it sit, then slowly draw some more." Next to us at the bar, two Irishmen attacked dinner plates filled with meat, big bowls brimming with mashed potatoes on the side. We left Louisburg in a traffic jam caused by sheep casually ambling down the road.

Driving to Galway, fearless drivers whizzed past us in pouring rain. Roads narrowed, giving us close encounters with rock walls on one side, buses and trucks on the other. Leo complained his hands were scraped from the fences.

Snug in bed at Jurys Hotel in Galway, I was awakened by noisy revelers yelling, "Free Beer, Free Beer!" Apparently a cold rain didn't dampen their spirits. The party-goers quieted down at dawn when the garbage trucks began banging through the streets. At breakfast I said, "The Irish had great "craic" last night." The word tickled Tyler when I explained that "craic" means fun,

The Irish designate rainy days as hard or soft. To get the feel of the climate in Ireland, turn on the shower and walk in and out several times. We'd wake up to sunshine shining through our windows—and walk out the door to rain. Walking hunched in our hooded raincoats, we'd realize the sun was out and unzipped in time for another shower forcing us to zip up again.

Today, TV had predicted it would be "showery and possibly thundery." We lucked out! After driving through hard rain, the sun came out as we parked at Cliffs of Moher. Looking forward to the unspoiled rugged Cliffs, we were horrified at seeing massive construction equipment, workers with orange vests swarming the area. A sign explained that a huge visitor's center was being built, with an estimated cost of thirty-six million. The old musty-smelling stone cottage gift shop we'd shopped in five years ago was gone, replaced with a fancy gift shop, a pricey restaurant, and a huge parking area.

The cliffs were breezy and misty, water swirling at the bottom of the rocks. Not as exhilarating as our first thunderous visit, but the high cliffs are still an imposing sight. We left with heavy hearts because the natural landscape was turning into a tourist trap. The village nearby had also expanded with this prosperity, but we laughed with delight when we saw cows grazing on a new golf course. "The cows aren't impressed!" Leo said. "I wonder if cow pies interfere with golf scores."

In Limerick, we hurried over for a quick tour of Folk Park Village in Bunratty Park on our way to the medieval banquet. Stone-floored cottages with thatched roofs ranged from a single room for the poorest farmers to several bedrooms for the blacksmith and doctor. The houses displayed the tools of the inhabitants, which made us happy for doctors' modern instruments. All houses had religious pictures on the walls and smelled of smoke from the peat fireplaces. Tyler chased the live chickens clucking around the cottages and a rooster strutting on top of an authentic stone fence.

Climbing stone spiral steps to the Bunratty Medieval Banquet, we were greeted by a Lord and Lady in Medieval costumes: "Welcome M'Lord, M'Lady." I have a framed photo of Lord Tyler posing with three pretty ladies-in-waiting.

Musicians entertaining in the center of the huge drawing room doubled as servers, keeping our pottery cups filled with robust red mead. Lady Josephine, a lovely dark-haired singer with beautiful eyes, served our table. When steaming bowls filled with creamy vegetable soup arrived with only a knife, we quickly sliced thick slices of brown bread to lap up the soup. Using our fingers, we grabbed greasy spare ribs and oven-browned potatoes from big bowls on the tables. For the main course, Lady Josephine filled plates with chicken and the plates were passed down the table from one person to the other until all were served.

After dessert, our wait staff became musicians again and we had a grand time listening to an Irish harpist, a fiddler, and several singers. Leaving the banquet, we joined other Americans at Durty Nelly's to enjoy Guinness and Baileys, but cautiously; I knew from experience that Durty Nellie's can play dirty tricks when having too much "craic."

We served ourselves an Irish breakfast from a buffet. The waitress came with coffee and Tyler turned the cup over for her; she said, "How observant you are—one hundred smacks for you." I wasn't sure what she meant by smacks, but when she was clearing off, he handed dishes to her and she said, "What a lovely young man."

We drove to Blarney Castle through rain on narrow, winding roads with trucks tearing past us. Blarney Castle is very old, covered with moss, and crumbling. Built in 1446 by Dermot McCarthy, Queen Elizabeth coaxed Lord McCarthy to will the castle to the Crown, but he refused with eloquent excuses and compliments. The Queen, not fooled by his smooth talk, exclaimed, "This is all Blarney. What he says he rarely means." Ever since, kissing the Blarney Stone is supposed to give the gift of gab.

We climbed one hundred twenty-seven slippery triangular stone steps spiraling up to the roof (battlement), and 'twas a battle to get up there. The narrow passageway got smaller and smaller. Jayne explained that they made small passageways to hide the children from invasions. "The soldiers couldn't get up there to kill the kids." Leo worried he wouldn't be able to squeeze through the small hole at the top. My legs were shaking when I got to the top, not from climbing, but from fear of slipping on the slick wet stones.

I declared, "I'm not lying down in the rain to kiss that stupid stone." Tyler was first, then Leo. Lying on their backs, they grabbed hand rails, put their heads back, and with a man holding their legs so they didn't fall off, they kissed the stone set in the wall below the battlements. Watching Jayne kiss the stone, I decided not to be chicken. Lying down, praying the man wouldn't let me fall, I hoped I'd get a bit of the Irish "gift of gab" so I can chime into the conversation at the Karsnia Sisters' gatherings!"

The trip down on another stairway was easier, but I gripped the railing tightly. Tyler disappeared into rooms on various levels, continuing his search for skeletons. There were phenomenal views of the wooded river valley from the top of the castle, and a grove of ancient yew trees declared to be a former site of Druid worship.

The streets of Blarney are very narrow with cars parked on both sides of the road, barely room for one car, but somehow two cars get through. Jayne adopted this same blasé attitude while I scrunched in the back seat with my eyes closed.

At the MayKerry Restaurant and Pub we enjoyed tasty seafood chowder, topped off with Bailey's cheesecake. The rural Ireland pub surprised us with a fancy restroom. The flusher was a large shiny silver circle embedded on the wall behind the toilet, and we washed our hands in washbowls on a lovely marble vanity.

Several tables of women celebrating a birthday filled the small dining room, savoring generous helpings of meat and mashed potatoes without a mention of calories. A gray-haired lady asked, "Will you take our picture?" They posed expectantly.

Jayne asked, "Where's your camera?"

"We don't have one. Can you use yours?" Our cameras were sitting on the table.

Jayne said, "But you won't get to see it."

The lady said, "That's OK. We want our picture to go to America."

Another piped up, "Maybe we'll see it in an American magazine."

Passing the camera around to see their pictures, they were as excited as children at seeing themselves. One said, "Mags, you look good." Mags (our friendly lady) preened and took another look.

I said, "Give me your address and I'll send it to you." Mags wrote her address on a napkins and I mailed her the pictures when I got home, disappointed not to get a response.

After shopping in the huge Blarney Woolen Mills, we walked into a small shop to get out of the rain. The lady shop owner said in a lilting Irish brogue, "The sun will be shining this afternoon. A girl is getting married and she rang up to see about the weather. The sun will shine."

Her husband told Leo that he had recently buried four friends, and it was pouring down rain for all four. "Our friends are dying off left and right." The sun was shining when we opened the door to leave and the shopkeeper looked up from folding clothes. "See, I told you."

Leaving Blarney, Jayne appreciated driving on a Dual Carriageway—for a short time. We drove slowly through construction on a major highway across the rolling hills. Posted signs said "Traffic Calming." Jayne said it meant to slow down—and we did. Prosperity slows traffic.

On our way to Rock of Cashel in Tipperary, past lush pasturelands, we caught glimpses of River Shannon, the longest river in Ireland. We'd driven through intervals of rain and sun and now, God stretched out a rainbow over the river.

Our speed demon was determined to get us to Cashel Castle before it closed, but we were minutes too late. Walking around the Romanesque castle with crumbling walls, we told Tyler the story we'd heard about St. Patrick on our last visit. Cashel was the center of power when St. Patrick baptized King Aengus in 432 AD, making Aengus the first Christian king in Ireland. Patrick is especially famous for explaining the mystery of the Trinity with a Shamrock. We wandered in the graveyard looking at toppled-over tombstones, names worn away from the centuries. Tyler searched, but didn't find a skeleton.

At The Legends, a charming hotel and restaurant located just below the castle, our hostess seated us in a pleasant room with a fireplace. Relaxing there, waiting for the waitress to call us into the dining room for dinner, we visited with a couple from Ohio who said, "We're touring Ireland for three weeks. We love Ireland and Guinness." In the small, charming dining room, the impeccably dressed tables with white tablecloths and vases of flowers set the ambience for superb squash soup, superb walnut salad, and superb salmon.

The next day, during a traffic jam in Mitchelstown, we watched pedestrians being buffeted by wind and rain, struggling to hold onto their umbrellas. The radio began playing, "Everywhere you go, take the weather with you." Laughing, we enjoyed watching the umbrella parade as we dawdled through main street for over an hour.

The speedometer needle was slowly moving out of coasting when Jayne spied cattle in a pasture heading for the highway. Flooring the gas pedal, she missed the sluggish cows by an inch. Wiping sweat off his forehead, Leo said, "Lucky cows. You would have creamed them."

Our tour around Ireland completed, we returned to Michael's house. He was waiting to take us on a tour of Dublin. "Times are booming. The terrible traffic and expensive parking make it cheaper and easier to take the Dart instead of driving. There's lots of construction to repair old buildings, add on, and build new." Riding high above the ground on the Dart, Leo counted fifty-four tower cranes.

Trinity College's cobblestones are a haven of quiet in noisy downtown Dublin. Michael gave Tyler (and me as I followed them around taking notes) an impressive history lesson about the Book of Kells. He said, "First, they had to kill the calf to make their paper, which is called parchment or vellum. They killed one hundred thirty-five calves to make the Book of Kells and then had to scrape off all the hair. They killed birds and used their feathers for pens."

It's my third trip to the Kells, but the first time I heard these details. Moving to another exhibit, Michael instructed, "Scribes and artists worked together on each page. They made the first letter on each page really fancy, decorating it with dragons and snakes, making it hard to read. Of course, they are written in Latin by the monks. The four Gospels were painstakingly illustrated by the monks in the fifth century." In the spectacular Long Room, Tyler was impressed that Michael had climbed up those ladders to get books.

Dublin Castle, located in the middle of town, is converted to government offices. And museums. And guess what! Success! A skeleton in the Museum of Natural History brought a huge smile on Tyler's face! After all his searching, Tyler jumped up and down, not at all disappointed at the tiny, shriveled up skeleton in a glass case.

River Liffey runs through the middle of Dublin, and we stood on the Ha'ppeny Bridge admiring it until intermittent rain squalls turned into pelting rain. Of course, being in the Temple Bar area, we stopped in Michael's favorite bar to get out of the weather. The TV was blaring loud enough to fracture our eardrums. Leaving the three guys, Jayne and I found a quiet coffee shop to enjoy Chai Tea.

Michael liked to attend the "express service" at Church of St. Monica. "I'm out in half an hour." This Sunday, he was the one who delayed it; he gave a speech asking for volunteers to deliver his newsletter, *St. Monica's Good News*. He cajoled "Not a big job. We bundled them according to the roads that people live on." The priest said he wished the Good News of the *Bible* would get out as effectively as the newsletters.

Michael had written a story about his grandmother Lizzie: "In my youth, I remember we cringed each time one of the 'good men of the parish' proclaimed the contributions in public at Christmas: 'Tommy Devlin five pounds; Lizzie Rice ten shillings.'" Michael was indignant. "The idea was, obviously, Tommy Devlin was a better Christian than Lizzie Rice. Tommy Devlin owned several pubs and Lizzie Rice was poor."

Michael loves telling tales about his grandmother. "Lizzie was left a widow at a young age and raised her five children as a single parent. She opened a store with a sack of potatoes and what today would be approximately fifty cents. Although wearing a Pioneer pin to show she supported Prohibition, she drank a pint of Brandy every day. I often went to the back door of the pub to ask for 'the wee parcel for Lizzie.'" Unfortunately, the Rice family liked horse racing, and Lizzie's son Johnny was a gambler. He lost a lot of Lizzie's money on the horses, and when Michael's mother, Maureen, took over the store she also supported his gambling.

We were surprised when Michael said that the IRA actually started in the USA. "Irish soldiers who fought in the Civil War came back and started the IRA. I went up into the attic above the store one day and saw Uncle Patrick sitting on the bed cleaning a gun, two grenades beside him. He was killed two years later."

Betty took us to Malachite Castle while Michael stayed home to cook dinner. The Great Hall in Malachite Castle is the oldest medieval room in Ireland. The entire castle and its antique furnishings have been remarkably preserved; one room has the original draperies. The upstairs bedrooms had lovely furnishings, and there were ancient toys in the children's rooms, many with a horse theme. From high turrets, we looked down at two hundred fifty acres beautifully landscaped.

Betty said, "The Talbot family lived in this castle for eight hundred years. Rose, the last living relative moved to Tasmania, but in 1973 she donated the castle to the town." In the Great Hall there are portraits of fourteen Talbot men who ate breakfast in the hall before leaving for the Battle of Boyne in 1690. None of them returned.

Irish history is filled with battles and wars!

Chapter 24
Newgrange Mystery
2006 continued

Michael put on his fedora—our guide was ready to take us to see an Irish mystery. Newgrange, built about 3000 B.C., is older than the Pyramids and Stonehenge.

On the way to the site, we walked across a bridge over the Boyne River in the Boyne Valley. Michael said, "This river valley was the cradle of Irish civilization. The Battle of the Boyne was fought here in 1688. Remember the fourteen Talbots from Malachite Castle killed in this battle? Protestants triumphed and this was the beginning of total Protestant power over Ireland. It ushered in the confiscation of Catholic lands for the next three hundred years."

I said, "That's why Leo's grandpa left Ireland in 1888—he wanted to own land."

The Newgrange guide said, "Newgrange is a passage grave that allows the spirit passage to the other life." He advised us that we would have to squeeze through a narrow passageway leading to a chamber that holds only twenty-four people, warning, "Claustrophobic people should not attempt it."

The mound has an elaborate entrance covered with quartz stones, an open window above it. On December 21, the Winter Solstice, rays of sun enter through the window at the entry, lighting up the burial chamber. The guide said, "If you want to be here for this phenomenon, you should put your name in the lottery. They draw twenty-four names; however, there's the possibility there will be no sun that day. Regardless of the gamble, people flock to sign up for the lottery." All twenty-four of us looked up at the window, amazed. How did they acquire such astounding wisdom five thousand years ago?

In the Newgrange museum, there's a picture of a monstrous boulder tied onto logs and historians assume this is how the natives hauled them to the site. Michael explained, "Mathematicians have estimated it would have taken eighty men about three weeks to haul them. They speculate that they had to be hauled from about seventy kilometers away." They created this feat with a few simple tools—and man power. Again, it's mind-boggling!

From Newgrange, Michael drove us to the town of Drogheda to see St. Lawrence Gate, a thirteenth century tower in the middle of town. Our personal historian said: "Oliver Cromwell attacked Drogheda in 1649 and slaughtered all the inhabitants. Oliver Plunkett was a Catholic archbishop and he was killed by hanging, drawing and beheading. This method meant hanging until almost dead, then revived, dragged through the streets and again revived. Then they disemboweled him while he was still alive and chopped off his head. Pope John Paul declared Oliver Plunkett a saint. Oliver's head is on display in Rome at St. Peter's Basilica." (I didn't know this story when I was in Rome, or I would have paid homage to Archbishop Plunkett.) Despite this gruesome story, the elaborate church had an exquisite rose window and an intricate organ.

I love Michael's version of another history lesson: "Brendan the Navigator sailed across the Atlantic and discovered America long before Christopher Columbus. But he kept it a secret, not like that blabbermouth Italian. St. Brendan was a sixth century monk who did a lot of traveling. Canadian Indians built canoes the same way as the Irish, the only two places in the world that built them like that."

Back at Michael's house, he donned his chef hat and served us a meal as good as any Thanksgiving dinner: turkey, oven potatoes, carrots, my favorite mushy peas and pink fluffy dessert. (He'd left instructions with Betty on how to finish preparing the meal he'd started.) Good food, good company, good "craic"! And now—another good-bye.

During the nine-hour flight to Minneapolis, I finished reading my book by the priest and author, Andrew Greely. After all, we're both authors who write about the Irish! In Minneapolis, we hugged and kissed Jayne and Tyler good-by.

Another "brilliant" trip filled with history, education, and scenery. Leo loves the Irish breakfasts and pints of Guinness. Jayne loves Irish people and thatched roof cottages. I love the green rolling fields criss-crossed with stone fences. Tyler loves the medieval castles and dungeons and searching for skeletons. We all love Michael and Betty.

Scandinavian Tour

Chapter 25
Scandinavian Tour—*Following the Flowers*
May 2000

Bonnie researched and organized a trip to Norway. "Are you interested? We'll be in Holland when the tulips bloom." Absolutely! Bonnie said her friends, Carol and Mary Lee, are blonde Norwegians and have never been to Norway, so they're raring to go. "Carol grew up with me in Big Falls, and Mary Lee became a good friend when she moved here a few years ago. She's young with lots of energy. Carol has a few medical problems, but she's fun, too."

On the bus ride from Heathrow, jet lagged and bedraggled after our long night of flying, we'd oohed and aahed over the huge pink and white cone-shaped flowers of the chestnut trees that lined the streets. London was the first stop on the eight-country tour for our group of four—Bonnie, Mary Lee, Carol, and me.

Grainne (rhymes with Sonia) O'Malley, our Grand European Tour leader, a tall woman with short sandy hair, twinkling eyes, and a friendly face met us in the lobby of Swallow International Hotel. Although Grainne was trying to shepherd thirty-three members of our group into hotel rooms, she didn't bat an eye when Bonnie loaded Carol, Mary Lee, and me into a taxi. Off we sped to Buckingham Palace for changing of the guard, our first adventure on this twenty-day tour.

At Buckingham Palace, weaving between deep crowds, we squirmed into a small opening at the black wrought iron gates tipped with gold. The Palace grounds, barren of landscaping, became a resplendent affair of red and black, flashing swords, drums, and snappy guards marching in formation.

Carol dashed into the street to get a close-up of a guard riding a horse, but a policeman shooed her back. Undaunted, she asked him to pose with her. The policeman, first making sure they were behind the rope barrier, put his arm around her and smiled widely for the camera.

Bonnie was holding the concierge captive when we returned to Swallow. Visibly shaken, he dialed theater after theater. Hard as he worked the phone, finding four tickets for the same play was impossible, and we agreed to take two tickets for *Les Miserables* and two for *Chicago*.

Relaxing on leather couches in the lounge after giving our credit card information to reserve our theater seats, we chatted with an English couple and their dogs. Barbara and Malcom had saved the two dogs from an abusive situation and were being honored by the Humane Society. Bonnie asked questions about Princess Di's death. Barbara answered, "We may never know what really happened. But, Prince Charles and Camilla seem very happy."

Energized from food, anxious to see London's famous department store, Bonnie and I took a bus to Harrod's. From the glittering statues of the Egyptian Room, guarded at the entrance by a gold Sphinx and a helmeted Bobby, Bonnie and I wandered, wide-eyed and open-mouthed, into the Edwardian Food Hall, the equally resplendent grocery department. Fish, meat, and poultry were displayed like precious jewels. We rode the escalators, agog at the gleaming state-of-the art appliances presented as objects d'art. Even the ironing boards were fit for a queen.

Bonnie approached a clerk dressed in a black suit with crisp white shirt and tie. "Can you cash a pound so we have change for the street car?" Staring at her as though she were crazy, he quickly recovered and politely said, "I'm unable to do that, but you can go to Harrods Bank downstairs." I'm sure he wondered what such scruffy specimens were doing in Harrods. let alone have business at the bank.

The teller in the bank looked thunderstruck when Bonnie poured out a bag filled with coins, asking him to sort them by country. Customers behind her swiftly switched lines. I edged away, pretending I didn't know her.

With Bonnie's banking taken care of, we rushed back to the hotel. Although nervous about splitting up, we sped off in two separate taxis to two different theaters. **Chicago's** gangsters and murderesses in the 1920s kept Carol and me awake despite our weariness from traveling all night. The musical is based on a play that was written by a woman reporter covering the trials of women who were being acquitted even though they committed homicides. When the lively music stopped, jet lag quickly replaced the synergy that had been surging through our veins during the energetic dancing and singing.

Slumping with fatigue, we watched countless cabs go by with smug-looking passengers peering out the windows as we dragged ourselves dejectedly down the sidewalk, which was as crowded as though it were noon instead of midnight. I wanted to sit on the curb and cry. We jumped when a man dressed in black stepped out from behind a parked car. "Taxi?"

"Yes!" We dragged ourselves into the car. Immediately after slamming the door I became uneasy. Most of the twenty thousand taxis in London are Mercedes, built specifically to be cabs, artfully painted with colorful advertising to help offset their cost. This car was black with a normal car interior.

"Swallow International," we told the Jamaican driver. He asked, "Where is hotel?" He scanned the brochure handed him, and then asked in broken English, "Do you have number to call?" Now I was nervous in earnest.

Carol fumbled around in the purse she'd purchased for the trip. Each time she tried to find something, she cursed, "Why did I buy this expensive purse?" Zipping and unzipping pockets, she finally found her hotel key with the name and telephone number. The driver said, "I call for address." He repeated instructions from the person on the other end of the phone in broken English over and over.

Recalling that wild taxi ride over winding dirt roads in the Caribbean, I felt similar panic, and peered over front seat looking for the meter. No meter. I asked the driver angrily, "Where is your meter?"

"I work for Coften Cars," the driver said, reaching back to hand me a card. "We have no meter, we're cheaper." Carol started haggling with him over the cost. I couldn't believe it—I was worried about my life; she was worried about the cost! I grabbed the door handle with sweaty hands, debating about jumping out while she haggled. I let go of the handle with a sigh of relief when I recognized the National Museum of Science, a huge building close to the Swallow. As we pulled into the hotel driveway minutes later, I ran for the hotel, leaving Carol haggling over the cost. I fell into bed after midnight, not looking forward to our 4:45 a.m. wake-up call to leave for Amsterdam.

* * *

We all felt skittish about traveling underwater on the Eurostar passenger train through "The Chunnel." To my surprise, I fell asleep during a long blackout, waking up from a blissful nap to see lush French countryside. In Brussels, we were hustled onto a motor coach to Holland without a chance to look around.

Zuiderzee! I love the sound of Zuiderzee! It resounded with me in elementary school and still does. Holland is Zuiderzee and windmills and dikes and, of course, tulips. Visions of endless fields of tulips and daffodils had determined our departure date in May. Researching extensively, Bonnie had assured us, "We'll be in Holland at Tulip Time!" But we were horrified by fields of headless green; farmers mow down tulips as soon as they bloom. This process provides nutrients to the marketable bulbs, protecting an eight billion-dollar business. Remember when you plant your bulbs—they were beheaded for you. Stunning carpets of red, yellow, pink, and purple blooms seemed even more resplendent when we did see fields not yet beheaded, and our displeasure at being shuttled out of Brussels without even a quick tour was all but forgotten as the magnificence restored our souls.

Windmills, dikes, and levees have been part of Dutch engineers and farmers' efficient agricultural system for thousands of years. Many workmen lost their lives when they built the Zuiderzee dike in 1932, starting at both ends—at the English Channel and at Holland. A statue commemorates the laying of the final stone when the two ends were brought together.

Taking a boat cruise through canals in the center of Amsterdam was a journey back to the seventeenth century. Bold colored homes with fancy gable roofs built by wealthy merchants during the Dutch Golden Age surround the canals. Boats recycled as homes are anchored inside the canals. White picket fences with trees and flowers poking out of pots turn the small houseboats into charming floating gardens in the middle of the murky water.

At Anne Frank Museum, we trudged up a narrow, steep stairway concealed behind a bookcase. Anne wrote on August 21, 1942: "Now our Secret Annex has truly become secret. Mr. Kugler thought it would be better to have a bookcase built in front of the entrance to our hiding place." Every year, eight hundred thousand visitors read Anne's history of the horrors of war.

From that fourth floor secret annex in Amsterdam, I looked out at a chestnut tree waving white cone-shaped flowers. Pondering Anne's poignant story, I wondered if this tree was her link to the outside world while she hid in terror of the Nazis. Did this tree stretch up to comfort the talented girl who wrote in her diary that it was difficult being cooped up, unable to go outside? Chestnut trees astounded us with their beauty in all the countries we visited, an alliance not halted by armed guards at borders.

Dejected from Anne's tragic story, we tramped Amsterdam's ancient cobblestones. Tired and hungry, our growling stomachs sent us searching for a restaurant. All chairs and tables were filled in every outdoor patio we passed. Finally, we saw some people leaving a table. Rushing over, we plunked down in the chairs, exhausted. My legs felt like they'd been pounded down to stubs. The waitress asked, "Did you get permission to sit here?"

"Permission?" Bewildered, we stared at the waitress.

Angrily, she asked, "Did you ask to sit here?" With blank faces, we shook our heads. "I'll check with the bartender."

A sweaty young man in a T-shirt came out shouting, "You cannot sit here. We are closed."

Looking around at all the tables filled with people, Bonnie answered, "Closed? There are lots of people here."

"Yes. See how I sweat? I cannot cook any longer. You must go."

Giving up, we wearily limped to a taxi stand. Poking her head into the cab, Bonnie asked, "Can you take us to Centraal Station?" The driver, a slim boy with dark short hair, nodded. Gratefully, we piled in.

Bonnie asked, "Will you drive us through the red light district?" The narrator on the boat tour had mentioned the red light district: "For four hundred years women have advertised their bodies in shop windows. They are dressed in lingerie or nothing at all and have become a tourist attraction." Hiding a grin, the driver nodded "Yes." Turning a corner, he exclaimed, "It's closed off. I can't get down the street." Throngs of people poured down the street, filling it from sidewalk to sidewalk. "Do you want to get out here or go to Centraal?"

Bonnie had the door open when I grabbed her arm. "Bonnie, we're carrying our passports and all our money. Remember what Grainne warned us about? Professional pickpockets!" Carol and Mary Lee agreed, and we instructed the driver to take us to Centraal Station.

Hoping the hotel we'd booked in Lelystad was comfortable, we found the train going to the Amsterdam suburb. Feeling like rag dolls, we flopped down on the bright green seats.

"There's the sign for Lelystad," Bonnie shouted. Bursting out the door, Bonnie yelled at a handsome couple walking by, "Is this Lelystad?" Barely breaking his long stride, the man said, "Yes." By the time we climbed down the train steps, the woman had dragged the man back to help us.

Esther, our kind stranger, offered to walk us to our hotel saying, "My husband and I travel extensively and always find helpful people; we try to be ambassadors also." As we walked, she told us that her husband grew up in Lelystad. "Amsterdam got too small and they had to make more land. His parents moved to this new suburb to have a house and garden instead of apartment living in Amsterdam. Lelystad is reclaimed land that once was under sea level, called polderland. It was originally started for poor people, but now well-do-do people have taken it over."

Grainne had talked about filling in the sea to make land. I told Esther, "This is interesting. Our government forbids us to build on land designated as wetlands; here, they make land from the sea."

Still starving, we hoped the Mexican bar at Lelystad Hotel served food, but the restaurant was closed. Drinking Margaritas, hungrily stuffing chips with Salsa dip into our mouths, we laughed when Bonnie exclaimed, "This is a great dinner! I love chips."

* * *

Although destroyed during the war, Hamburg is one of the wealthiest cities in Germany, Located on River Alb, it's an industrial city with ports and shipping, engineering and printing, beer breweries and media. It's a sign of prestige to commute to work by boat. Workers eat lunch in the green parks circling the river, watching sailboats on River Alb. Mercedes cars populate the parking lots.

We were barely out of urban traffic in Hamburg when I saw black and white cows grazing on green fields. Smiling to myself at this unexpected rural scene, I breathed in, hoping to smell the lilac bushes and wild roses blooming beside the road.

In Lubeck, Germany, we marched into Old Town through the same red brick gate built in the 1200s to tax peasants coming to town to sell their produce. During those medieval times, wealthy merchants built beautiful buildings and churches by taxing the poor. Modern buildings fill in empty spaces that were bombed, mingling with Medieval buildings. Marian Kirche, a church built in medieval times, was partially destroyed in World War II by bombs on a Palm Sunday. The bell that fell from the tower is still on the floor as a reminder of the damage done by wars. Silently condemning bombers for destroying a church on Palm Sunday, suddenly I felt like I'd been hit by a bomb. I was in Germany. Had my country bombed this town, forcing people to run to shelters?

Walking under a long curved canopy over age-old cobblestones, pealing church bells eerily transported me back in time. I imagined myself wearing a monk's robe, arms tucked in the sleeves, chanting prayers.

* * *

In Copenhagen, Denmark, the streets were buzzing with people: smooth-shaven men in business suits and bearded men in T-shirts, mingling, enjoying drinks in the setting sun in picturesque Nyhavn. Hans Christian Andersen's home is one of the colorful seventeenth century homes surrounding Nyhavn Canal.

Reading Hans Christian Andersen stories when I was a schoolgirl had given me a burning desire to visit Holland and I scrambled off the bus to see the Little Mermaid overlooking Copenhagen's harbor! Dare I say that I wasn't truly impressed? We have a similar mermaid on Rainy Lake that's nearly as beautiful—even though she's made from plain old rock, not bronze.

In Tivoli Gardens, music floating through the air added to the magical ambience. Tramping through the gardens with splashing fountains, four hundred thousand blooming flowers, and trees trimmed with one hundred ten lights, I was enchanted until too pooped to look at another bloomin' flower.

Exhausted from Tivoli, Bonnie ordered a brandy at the Hotel Imperial bar. Holding out her hand filled with coins, she said, "Take what I owe you for my brandy."

The bartender picked out some coins and said, "Those are not ours."

Looking down at the coins, Bonnie asked, "Well, what are they?"

"Those two are American."

Everyone burst into laughter as she innocently asked, "They are?" After inspecting them closer, she decided they looked familiar. "We've gone through a lot of countries, who can remember everything?"

Denmark is a rich country. We toured castles filled with awesome jewels, paintings and antiques. Copenhagen's Rosenborg Slot (castle), now a royal museum in the middle of the city, has lavish displays of Danish crown jewels and relics. The queen has a walk-in jewelry box filled with diamonds, sapphires, and emeralds. Rosenborg's Long Hall holds one of the world's largest collections of eighteenth century silver furniture. Three life-size silver lions, representing power, guard a king's coffin.

Frederiksborg Slot, one of the greatest Renaissance castles in northern Europe, is sited across three islands. An organ built in 1610 is still played during church services in the ornate chapel. Kronborg Castle at Helsingor, also known as Hamlet's Castle, features a bust of Shakespeare because it was possibly the setting for *Hamlet*. We were intrigued by the huge moat surrounding the castle. Frederik II originally built the fortress between 1574 and 1585 to collect taxes from Swedish ships on their way to the Baltic Sea.

Driving through the Danish Riviera we watched people strolling on the beach despite a chilly wind. Playing a game of choosing houses we'd want to buy, we were flabbergasted when Grainne said that the houses each cost about two million dollars. Reinforcing the fact that Denmark is wealthy, she said, "Some people in Denmark have lots of money."

My granddaughter, Jackie, attended Providence College in Rhode Island; Denmark reminded me of Rhode Island—it's really small and everybody lives close to the sea. Wealthy people in Newport, Rhode Island, also live in sprawling mansions overlooking the ocean.

Back in Amsterdam, we met a friend of Bonnie's for dinner. Karen, a relative of Blanche and Charlie Williams in International Falls, had worked at their Kettle Falls Resort with Bonnie. Now a medical doctor, Karen met us at Kanalen Restaurant. The head chef, Karen's cousin Arsmus, gave Karen a big hug. Chef Arsmus said they have high standards at Kanalen because their goal is to receive the Michelin Star. The menu offered a choice of three, four, five, or six course meals. We ordered from the three-course-menu but the chef sent out six incredible courses, including roasted fish served with Norwegian lobster stockfish.

We gave Chef Arsmus our personal Michelin Star for the best gourmet meal we'd ever eaten!

Leaving in the morning, we caught our last glimpse of what Grainne called "an airy city," a last glimpse of narrow cobblestone streets filled with colorful, tall, skinny houses snuggled side by side framing canals, and green parks.

* * *

Sweden, one of the richest countries in Europe, has lush forests with road signs warning "Watch for Moose." Large farmhouses perch on rolling hills with meadows of wildflowers. We stopped for "tea and wee" at a yellow restaurant on a hill overlooking a sparkling blue lake. Relaxing in sunshine on the patio, we begged to stay longer, but Grainne heartlessly loaded us back on the bus.

Stockholm is a beautiful city built on fourteen islands. Walking on Klarabergsgatan Street, the long names on the street signs confused us and we hailed a taxi to take us back to First Hotel. Our friendly driver turned off his meter to give us a mini-tour of Gamla Stan, the oldest section of Stockholm. When his wife called his cell, he said, "I can't talk now. I'm driving the Americans." Flowers spilled out of window boxes on the tall, brightly-painted apartment buildings preserved from the 1600s—another journey back in time. Knowng his wife would ask how much he made "driving the Americans," we insisted on giving him some money.

Cruising down the river on a Sunday afternoon, the boat took us under fifteen bridges linking the fourteen islands making up Stockholm. On all fourteen islands, people were walking and jogging, relaxing on benches in the sunshine, lying in the green grass beside beds of tulips and pansies, or enjoying outdoor concerts. City dwellers in the Scandinavian countries live outdoors after the long dark winter, and the unusually warm weather brought them out to enjoy life. In northern Minnesota, we're just as excited to get outdoors, plant flowers, and launch our boats to shake off winter blues.

Outdoor landscapes compete with indoor foodscapes in Sweden. Breakfasts in Scandinavian hotels are more elaborate than American motels' Continental breakfasts. Our first tour every day was around the Scandinavian breakfast buffet. Each long table was devoted to one type of food: The cold food table displayed large crystal bowls of cereals, Yogurt, and jam. A table filled with baskets of pastries and breads has a knife to cut your favorite slice. One table was devoted to fish: herring in assorted sauces, salmon and shrimp presented intact with heads and staring eyes. (I didn't find them appetizing first thing in the morning.) Caviar squeezed out of a tube like toothpaste. Cold cuts and cheeses took up another table. The hot choices were boiled eggs, scrambled eggs, bacon, sausage, and potatoes. Everywhere, the coffee was strong! One cup and the caffeine lasted all day.

* * *

The city of Bergen, Norway, welcomed us with pink and red rhododendrons bursting through fences and Edvard Grieg music in the air. It also introduced us to its incessant rainfall by drenching us as we carefully trod slippery cobblestone streets. Lace curtains and bright red geraniums decorate the rural windowsills.

On Norway's Flam Railway spiraling through tunnels up a mountain, the train ride reveals breathtaking views of waterfalls catapulting into raging rivers. Blissfully focusing our cameras, we clicked, but instead of the magnificent view, we'd photograph blackness as we sped through another dark tunnel. Engineering genius forged tunnels through mountains, opening up formerly inaccessible "Jewels of Norway."

Trading the Flam train for Fjord Lord, we cruised on Aurlands Fjord under towering mountains providing spectacular vistas. The tranquil blue fjords reflected watery paintings of lush green forests turned upside-down in mirror-like waters. Staring up at the vertical sides of the mountain, we wondered how farmers got to the top. Grainne said, "Children and animals have to be tethered to keep them from falling off."

Norway's icy-blue glacier, Boyabreen, hovers on the snowy tundra of Hardanger Plateau, a stark contrast to the fjords. Grainne entertained us with stories of trolls being zapped by sun rays and turning into stones as we drove over the wintry mountains. Scrubby trees grow like gnarled old men on Norway's moors, but flowers defying the cold grow on grassy sod roofs.

Grainne, had promised, "Geiranger will be a highlight. We'll be there on May 17th to celebrate Syttende Mai—Norwegian Independence Day. This is the most colorful and festive day of the year in Norway." Bonnie, Carol, and Mary Lee, my co-travelers of Norwegian descent, quivered with anticipation. They were getting back to their roots.

Grainne's favorite British slang word whenever we saw something spectacular—"gobsmacked!—became our favorite adjective. I was "gobsmacked" by my own personal Syttende Mai.

Chapter 26
Syttende Mai
May 2000 continued

Cuddling under the soft duvet, I cherished the contrast of sumptuous splendor inside my room in Union Hotel while listening to roaring waterfalls outside. Stretching, relishing the luxury of dozing instead of travelling before dawn, ten days after leaving London, Geiranger felt like paradise.

During the 50-minute ferry ride, the only transportation to the remote island of Geiranger, standing on the deck in a light sprinkling of rain, I watched endless waterfalls cascading down the mountains. Everybody rushed out on deck to count The Seven Sisters, the largest and most famous waterfalls, and were rewarded with a rainbow of pink, yellow, blue, and green.

The owner of Union Hotel greeted us warmly. A fourth generation of the Mjelva family, he proudly told us about this first class hotel that had been built four hundred years ago in the majestic mountains and deep fjords.

Carol and I gasped when we opened the door to a charming room, a welcome sight for weary travelers. Red sofa and chairs in the seating area invited us to plop down and gaze in wonder out of three large windows framing a spectacular view. Two mountain peaks are divided by a cascading ribbon of water twisting and turning through green forests, disappearing, then reappearing further down the hill as a raging river. The sound of waterfalls was soothing after a week of clamoring traffic and shrill sirens. Opening a window to the pure mountain air, we relaxed in front of the stunning vista, unable to take our eyes off the view.

In the dining room, round tables were filled with incredible food. One displayed assorted breads; one displayed a fish tier with crawdads, shrimp, lobster, crab legs, salmon and herring; one displayed hot foods;

one displayed meats, and last, but not least, one displayed tempting desserts.

Hours later, stomachs stuffed, we sank down in the lounge that stretched the length of the hotel. Snug groups of couches in solid red or with green and red stripes were arranged throughout the long room, offering a full view of snow-capped mountains. Water winding in never-ending motion poured down the mountains.

In the morning, our first tour of the day around the Scandinavian breakfast buffet, was comparable to the dinner buffet. I flipped pancakes on a large grill while Carol filled a plate with salmon, crackers, and Caviar. I avoided looking at Mary Lee's plate heaped with herring, relishing her Norwegian heritage.

"The parade starts at 10:30," Bonnie reminded us, eyes glowing with excitement. Syttende Mai, celebrated like our Fourth of July, commemorates the day Norway adopted its national constitution. From 1442 until 1814, Denmark ruled Norway. Denmark was forced by the Treaty of Kiel to cede Norway to Sweden. The Norwegians refused to recognize the treaty, and on May 17, 1814, they adopted a national constitution based on the U.S. democratic model. Although it wasn't until 1905 that Norway finally obtained its own monarch and its own flag, they continue to celebrate May 17th as their independence day.

On our way to the parade, we stopped on a bridge to gush at the gushing water spraying down from the mountain to the road, and then I walked further down the hill toward the harbor where I'd enjoyed my early morning walk, admiring the houses with wide wood doors, doors that opened just inches away from the road. Windows were decorated with lace curtains and colorful plants filled the windowsills. Yellow and red tulips tenaciously grew in a narrow strip of soil beside the winding road.

Finally, the band played and the parade started! Young and old marched behind the band, led by a Norwegian flag bearer. Young children wearing big grins enthusiastically waved miniature red Norwegian flags. Women wore traditional costumes: black dresses (bunads), decorated with yellow, blue and green embroidery and glittering brooches and necklaces. Men and boys wore black suits. Umbrellas popped open when showers immediately rained on the parade, adding color among the marchers. Bonnie asked, "We're Norwegian. May we join your parade?"

Bringing up the rear, we followed the parade to the church, waiting in the foyer as the Lutherans settled into simple wooden pews. The choir led the congregation in the gathering hymn, the minister lit a candle with the opening prayer, but, unable to understand his Norwegian sermon, we quietly left. While walking back to the hotel, the sun came out and I quickly changed to hiking shorts.

Feeling adventurous, I followed a road uphill. Perched on a rock atop a hill in Norway, I beheld the wonders of God. Far below, the blue fjord carved out by ancient glaciers sliced the earth. Starting like shiny silver ribbons high in the mountain peaks, the falling water widens as it snakes down the face of the mountain to replenish the fjord. The water splashes up to green shores where horses graze and baby lambs frolic after their mothers. Monopoly-sized farmhouses in traditional Norwegian colors of blue, red, and yellow are colorful dots on the velvety green patches divided by darker green forests.

Sitting there in the midst of such beauty, a Norwegian flag flapping above me, waves of patriotism overwhelmed me and I hummed *America the Beautiful*.

Closing my eyes, soaking in the atmosphere, listening to birds sing, water splashing, raging rapids swirling up a mist—I converted to Norwegian-ism. Although it didn't take much because my best friend Maxine was Norwegian and their home was my second home as I was growing up, her mother, Borg, my second mother. While attending St. Olaf College, I sometimes thought I was Norwegian, but it didn't include Lutefisk!

Gunshots! I nearly toppled off my rock. My heart thudding, I looked around in panic before realizing the loud bangs must have been fireworks or guns shot off in celebration.

When my heartbeat slowed, remembering Mr. Mjelva's story about World War II, I thought about soldiers marching through this peaceful country. The Nazis took over the Union Hotel in 1941, forcing the present owner's grandfather to flee. Norway exchanged tranquility for terror.

Thinking I should join Bonnie, Carol, and Mary Lee, I wandered down to city hall. Mothers still dressed in their fancy Norwegian dresses were supervising children playing outside. Feeling conspicuous in bike shorts, I walked past the hall, continuing up the road to discover another paradise!

I ventured through a big wooden gate with owls carved into the thick posts at Geiranger Nature Park. A troll carved out of a tree beckoned to me from a little garden, a waterfall spraying in the midst of the flowers.

Following misty paths through the woods, clicking my camera constantly, picturesque scenes unfolded before me. Each waterfall gushed longer, wilder, and more thunderous.

I saw a head bobbing in the water! Stopping to stare, I realized the mermaid splashing among boulders was a wooden water sprite. In a whirlpool below a rushing waterfall, the swirling water made it look real, though not as polished as Copenhagen's sophisticated mermaid. Heart racing in excitement, I sat down to enjoy these stupendous surroundings. As dinner time approached, I reluctantly left my magical paradise.

At City Hall, Bonnie, Carol, and Mary Lee were learning some facts from a schoolteacher. "The permanent population of Geiranger is two hundred fifty, but it swells to six hundred thousand in the summer. There are bad snowstorms in the winter, with occasional avalanches, so there's no skiing. But we enjoy socializing—and the peace." Bonnie, who had looked forward to eating rommegrot (a Norwegian cream pudding), complained that it tasted like paste. I commented, "Of course, it's made with flour and water; it *is* paste."

That evening, Union Hotel served an elegant sit-down dinner of salmon on lettuce, lamb, scalloped potatoes floating in butter, and a mixed vegetable medley of turnips, carrots, broccoli, and tomatoes. A decadent chocolate cake garnished with strawberries and slathered with brandy sauce was presented with dots of chocolate and raspberry sauce on the plate circling the cake.

By bedtime, we were stuffed to the max with both food and beauty. In the morning, furtively watching Mary Lee savor herring and a hearty Norwegian breakfast, I ate Yogurt. Perhaps I hadn't become a full-blooded Norwegian!

We had one last glimpse of enchanting Geiranger from the ferry, feeling we were stepping out of a fairytale. A fairytale of a simple life filled with national pride, with the beauty of unspoiled nature, with waterfalls and fjords, mermaids and trolls, peace and serenity.

Seven countries later—England, Belgium (that quick glimpse of Brussels), Holland, Germany, Denmark, Sweden, and Norway—we were back in London. Rush hour traffic stalled our bus, giving the tour guide time to stuff our heads with historic landmarks as we crawled at snail's pace to the Swallow. Wearily, we abandoned thoughts of any more sightseeing. When Bonnie descended on the concierge, he surrendered immediately and attached himself to the phone. Magically, two cancellations popped up for *Mama Mia*, a play highly recommended by the concierge. Carol and I chose seats for *Les Miserables* because Bonnie and Mary Lee had given it fabulous reviews.

Our tickets reserved, Bonnie told the taxi driver, "I want a real English pub where we can eat fish and chips with Londoners." He drove us to the Hand and Racquet Pub, a smoke-filled bar as small as the authentic Cheers bar in Boston. Choking in the thick cigarette smoke, I gladly tramped up a narrow, steep staircase into an empty room with three tables and a tiny bar in the corner. The only evidence that we were in a restaurant was a blackboard announcing "Today's Specials."

Pushing up a hinged section of the bar, the short, stocky bartender came out with menus. Introducing himself as Mick, he gave a wide toothless grin when we said his name suited him. The fish and chips came from somewhere via dumb waiter. Looking around the untidy eating area, I refused to worry about creepy things in the kitchen. Eating the bland fish and chips, washing the grease down with Miller beer, I ignored thoughts of cholesterol. Luckily, the only reason we needed the grungy restroom was to wash the grease off our hands.

In Piccadilly Circus, we frequently stopped pedestrians for directions to our theatres. Frowning, the person would pause before pointing the way. Later, I understood why— there are forty-three theatres in London's West End.

In Leicester Square, we ran into a blockade of people standing as though waiting for a parade. Overhearing whispers of "film star," Bonnie asked, "What film star?" Voices from the crowd chanted, "John Travolta. John Travolta is coming!"

Carol said, "I wouldn't mind missing part of the play to see John Travolta!" But we hustled her away, assuring her we wouldn't see anything in that solid wall of people. A few blocks later, roars from the screaming fans announced Travolta's arrival.

When we reached the Palace Theatre marquee advertising *Les Miserables,* Bonnie and Mary Lee continued walking until they found Prince Edward theatre featuring the new London musical, *Mama Mia.* When I saw the movie, I really wished I'd seen the London play! We often sang the song while exercising at Curves—it was so happy and bubbly!

Carol and I sat down in our excellent seats just in time to hear Jean Valjean, the star of the show, sing his opening prologue. We thought the first act of *Les Miserable's* was depressing because the French poor had terrible living conditions in the early nineteenth century. In the second act, I choked down tears when the students were all killed, but sobbed when the young boy was shot. However, a (fairly) happy ending, the superb acting and singing, and the revolving stage with awesome set changes combined to make it another memorable evening.

The historic Palace Theatre built in 1891 had plumbing that was more than miserable. Imagine a posh theater with snooty ladies in expensive dresses queuing up at the loo during intermission to hear: "It won't flush."

Leaving the theater at midnight, we encountered throngs of people sauntering the streets as though it were daylight. We moaned and groaned, watching the cabs speeding past us filled with passengers A yellow bicycle pulled up beside us as we stood on a curb looking like lost puppies. "Howdy," the bicyclist greeted us.

We stared at the strange-looking bicycle with two seats on the back. Carol asked, "Are you a cab?"

The tall, young Australian answered, "Yes. But I'm more expensive than a cab—I charge 20 pounds."

"It's too far for you to pedal," I said. "We're staying at Swallow International."

"You'll never get a cab here. Hop on. I'll drop you at the Ritz. Taxis will pick you up at the Ritz because they think you're rich." We climbed into the two passenger seats, so low I expected my butt to drag on the ground. Pedaling furiously, zigzagging around taxis and busses, our bicyclist zipped through red lights and careened over curbs onto sidewalks, scaring pedestrians. Screeching as though we were on a roller coaster, Carol and I hung on with white knuckles.

Our driver kept up a friendly conversation, scaring us more as he looked back to talk. "My name is Simon. I just moved to London from Australia six months ago. There are only thirty bicycle cabs in London—they're called cob cabs. When Simon stopped in front of the Ritz, I nearly stepped in front of a red double-decker bus. Simon said, "Get back on. I'd better drive you across the street so you get there safely." Delivering us across the street, Simon agreed to being paid with American money. "Sure. I'm going to Las Vegas in a couple weeks." A "real cab" picked us up a few minutes later.

Safe at the Swallow, I swallowed the lump in my throat. I had survived another wild adventure.

* * *

Returning safely home in time for northern Minnesota's late spring, I was welcomed by my own flowering lilac trees and a fragrant bouquet of blooms on the table.

A new rock garden of yellow and red tulips in my back yard reminds me of that springtime Scandinavian trip when we were "gobsmacked" as we followed flowers throughout Europe.

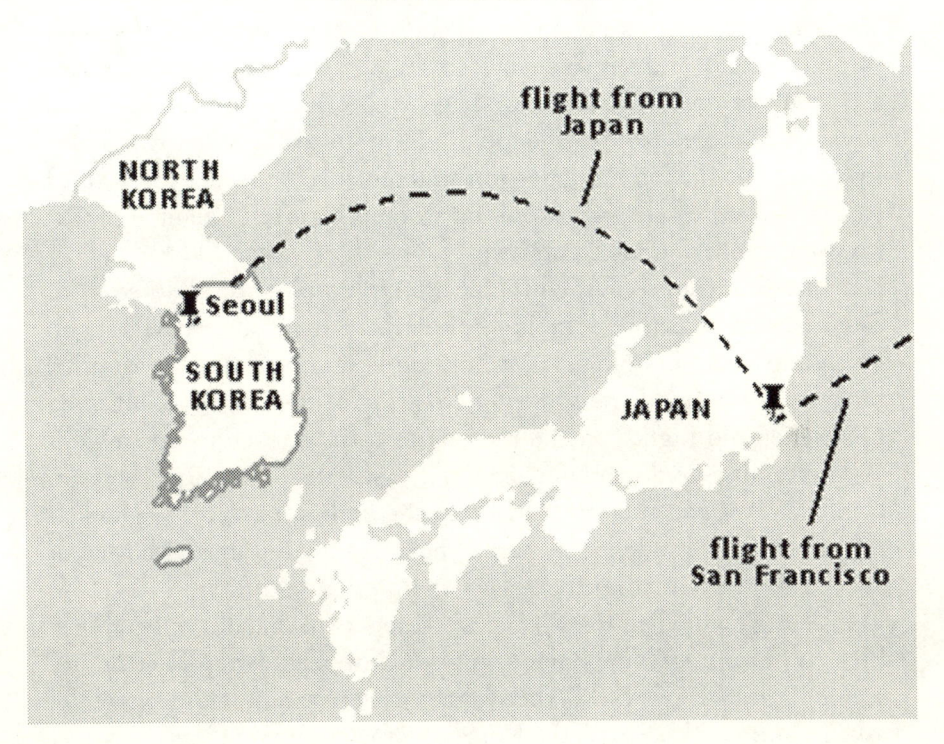

South Korea

NORTH KOREA

Seoul

SOUTH KOREA

flight from Japan

JAPAN

flight from San Francisco

Chapter 27
Asian Adventure
2004

I acquired great respect for Buddhism on my trip to South Korea.

Buddhist temples are many-splendored structures! Koreans love primary colors, and the ancient temples are alive with color. Koreans are proud of their temples, and scrupulously maintain their places of worship. Donnie's Korean friend Park drove us to a temple my first day in Seoul, but the big red gates to the temple were locked. However, I was fascinated by the fierce-looking wooden figures of giant "guards" towering over the temple entrance.

Towering giants guarded the next temple we visited and I stopped to admire them before climbing hundreds of steps up to pavilions on ascending levels. In each pavilion, a Buddha sits on an altar surrounded by lesser statues and the soothing chanting of monks. We continued up, higher and higher on the mountain until we overlooked treetops and skyscrapers in downtown Seoul. I'm fascinated by the juxtaposition of the ancient and the modern. From the highest pavilion, we looked down at rows of modern cars parked next to a storage area with rows of ancient brown Kimchi pots,

Feeling compelled to join the worshippers in one of the pavilions, I tossed my clunky New Balance into the jumble of fancy stilettos and strappy sandals. "How did the women get up here in those shoes?" I asked Donnie. He shrugged. "Korean women dress well."

Stepping into the pavilion, I took a mat from the huge pile in the corner and sat down cross-legged to observe the Buddhists for a few minutes, admiring their flexibility as much as their reverence. Imitating them, I stood straight, bowed my head, kneeled, stretched out my arms on the floor in front of me, and placed my forehead on my hands. Rose, our guide on the Seoul City Tour, had said that she assumes this position one hundred eight times before her university tests, but two prayers were enough for me. I decided Catholics have it easy: sit, stand, or kneel.

Leaving this sacred place, we were assaulted by noise—blaring horns on the streets, blaring music in the restaurants, shrill chatter on the subway. Agitated by the noise, head pounding, I longed to return to the soothing sounds of chanting monks. In Donnie's apartment, I sank down in a recliner, heaving a sigh of relief.

Although I'd never thought about going to Asia, it struck me that I couldn't miss a terrific opportunity to go while my brother was teaching at Foreign Language University. Timing was right. During the ten days I was there, he was off work for seven days—two weekends and three days for Chusok, the Korean Thanksgiving. The three days he worked, I recharged my batteries while pounding keys on his computer, downloading photos and journaling our busy schedule.

I knew I might not like the food from the questions Donald asked while planning our agenda before my arrival: Do you like spicy food? Do you like duck? Can you use chopsticks? Can you sit on the floor to eat? My answer to all of the above was a resounding "No!" Worse, people warned me, "Koreans eat dogs."

Saturday, my first day there, we ate lunch at a restaurant with a name that meant "Like a Flowing River." Donnie's friend, Park, said there are two hundred recipes for Kimchi, made from fermented cabbage. Besides Kimchi, Koreans relish radishes—served pickled, shredded, sliced, and diced.

At a traditional restaurant for dinner, while slipping my shoes off at the doorway, I watched the waiter put mats on the floor beside a low table. No wonder Korean people are slim! Sitting on the floor with my stomach scrunched up, I didn't have room for food. Soon my bum felt numb, my back and legs aching.

Koreans have many extra side dishes with every meal. Park called them—"weeds." I couldn't pick up anything with the chopsticks, so Park requested a fork; the fork picked up too many weeds. The waiter brought out a whole stewed chicken on a platter, so white that looking at it made me nauseous. There we sat, looking at the naked white chicken until Park jumped up and ran to the kitchen. Our waiter returned wearing white gloves; placing the platter of chicken on the next table, the waiter sat on the floor, and pulling clear disposable gloves over his white gloves, he tore the chicken apart. The tasteless chicken served with Kimchi and weeds gave me hope of losing weight.

At every meal I asked, "Is this dog?" Finally, Donnie told me to look at the doors of restaurants. "See that pig? That means they serve meat from pigs. A picture of a chicken means they serve chicken. I wouldn't take you to a restaurant that served dog." Good!

Donnie's friend, Carol, saved me from starvation when she invited us to dinner to meet Donnie's friends. How she cooked a turkey dinner in that small Korean kitchen is more than I know, but it was served with jokes and laughter, and without weeds!

Elderly women wearing mismatched tops and trousers crouch down amidst their produce on city sidewalks, trying to eke out a living, making me sad. "It's hopeless. How can they sell anything sitting side by side with the same fruit, the same vegetables, the same ugly fish, and the same strange things that look like twigs?" Recipes for medicinal twigs and herbs have been handed down from generation to generation.

Often, a man would stop, smile at me, and give a little bow. I told Park, "Koreans must like Americans. They bow to me." He said, "We respect the elderly." I glared at him, but restrained myself from ranting about how rude they are on the street. Crunched in the crowds, I was forced to dodge out of the paths of pedestrians—nobody ever stepped out of my way. Teenagers stride past the "aunts" hunkered on the street, ignoring them. Donnie pushed me out of the way of bicycles and motorcycles wheeling down the sidewalk. We dodged cars parked on sidewalks, too. Cars don't worry about pedestrians and pedestrians don't worry about cars. Watching every step I took was exhausting.

Knowing that I love rocks and exercise, Park planned a day of mountain climbing at Mt. Achasan. Boulders of varying sizes form the mountain, apparently lying where the glaciers dropped them. Climbing was nerve-racking. There were hordes of hikers racing up, almost shoulder to shoulder. Expert climbers darted around me, startling me as I concentrated on each step I took on the uneven rocky path. Luckily, there were frequent observation points where we could stop to get our breath and enjoy the fabulous view.

About halfway up, we found a comfortable spot by Jungnangcheon Stream. Park's wife had packed a picnic lunch of leftover Chusok food. Sitting on giant boulders in the sunshine beside a sparkling stream, celebrating Chusok solitude in superb rocky scenery—*Life is good!*

During Korea's five thousand year history, they have been invaded over nine hundred times, mostly by the Japanese. The Japanese annexed Korea in 1910. Rose, our tour guide, said, "They put up a huge government building, deliberately blocking the view of downtown Seoul's Kyongbok Palace, which Koreans love to see." I toured three of the five palaces in Seoul, all with elaborate landscaping, tiled roofs, and painted buildings.

The King was King! Over six hundred servants took care of his needs and protected him. The King's bedroom was a separate building in the middle of the palace grounds, numerous buildings surrounding it. Inside, servants' bedrooms surrounded his bedroom, resembling a maze for further protection. The queen and concubines lived in another building built in the same manner. The King chose which of his queens he visited at night. The servants were all segregated; boys and girls were not allowed to mingle. Of course, the girls hoped to be chosen by the King for his harem.

Koreans are extremely superstitious. Proudly, the guides pointed to the surrounding mountains that protect them. Animals protect them too, and stone statues of animals are placed at entrance gates. At Kyongbok Palace, because invaders destroyed it many times with fire, Koreans built in more protectors: A stone phoenix represents water to prevent fires; a tiger-like statue is pounced, ready to eat fire; and figures of the Zodiac on the roofs add further protection. To assure harmony with nature, the roofs of the buildings are green to match the leaves on the trees and the pillars are brown to look like tree trunks.

In the Korean Folk Museum, exhibits depict Korean life during many centuries. Mannequins wearing traditional clothing pose inside models of houses. It was astonishing to see how thoughtfully they designed houses centuries ago, with water piped into the house. Homes of well-to-do people had a kitchen, a pantry, and a housewife's room all in a row. The housewives tended the fire. I thought the Korean heating system innovative, with fires below the house under layers of stone and clay; yellow paper covers the floors. Koreans sit and sleep on the floor—to keep warm.

According to Richard Soccone's guidebook, *Travel Korea Way*, "The Korean Folk Village is a good way to learn about Korean culture, customs and people." It was especially interesting on Tuesday, September 28th, because it was Chusok, the Korean Thanksgiving. Koreans love wearing their traditional costumes for holidays, delighting in their own history.

Koreans are family-oriented, often stopping to take pictures of their children. They humbly nodded "Yes" when I pointed to my camera, asking permission to take a picture of their children simultaneously with them.

The village is set up as a traditional Korean country town with buildings representing designs of differing regions and lifestyles. The smell of roasting chestnuts over an open fire tantalized Donnie into buying a sackful from the woman in traditional costume. In a picnic pavilion we peeled off the shells, savoring the warm nuts. At the next table, a family was enjoying a picnic; smiling shyly, the mother came over to offer us rice cakes. Donnie ate several with relish; I ate one to be polite.

Unyielding crowds prevented me from seeing some performances. At the Acrobatics performance, I only caught glimpses of girls as they flew in the air on swings. Finally, getting gutsy, I squeezed my way into the front row at the Traditional Wedding Ceremony. Taking pictures of the groom sitting at the wedding table waiting for his bride, I was startled when hens on the table turned their heads. I stood staring—were they really alive? They were. Hens bring good luck. A duck, representing fidelity, was also a guest on the wedding table.

The bride entered with a bridesmaid on each side holding a veil over her face. One of the bridesmaids brought small bowls of wine to the bride and groom, each seated on opposite sides of the banquet table. When the ceremony was over, they marched off together.

Palaces and temples, museums and art exhibits, all introduced me to Korean history and culture. The play *Cookin' Nanta,* as the publicity promised, was "A percussive symphony of flying food and flashing blades." Supposedly preparing a wedding feast, four chefs energetically beat their make-shift percussion instruments while chopping, mixing, or baking. Knives on chopping blocks provided intriguing drum music.

The contrast of ancient with modern was fascinating. Modern skyscrapers loom over palaces built in the thirteenth and fourteenth centuries. Korean guides speak about harmony—sky, earth, and water—and their paintings represent harmony with the sun and moon, trees and mountains. While clinging to their traditions, South Koreans embrace modern technology. Although almost destroyed during the Korean War, Seoul has become a leading metropolitan city.

Without my brother's insistence that I visit him, I would not have experienced this Asian adventure. Without his guidance, I would not have experienced the Korean culture so intensely.

Chapter 28
Fearful Feng Shui
2004 continued

After a week of awesome sights in Seoul, we settled down in reserved seats on a bullet train to Gyeong-ju. Donnie had hired a guide and Mr. Kim met us at the train station carrying a sign with DONALD printed in big letters. Introducing himself, he morphed into a teacher. "I teach you Korean culture and Korean philosophy." I listened intently to his fractured English, trying to understand yin and yang, harmony and Feng Shui.

Mr. Kim explained that Feng Shui originated in China over three thousand years ago and is believed to use the laws of both heaven and earth to help one improve life by receiving positive forces, promoting harmony, the basis of Korean culture. Feng Shui is used to balance buildings and provide harmony. Chinese medicine uses yin and yang to balance the body.

Thousands of steps later, after climbing up to temples scattered in the mountains and viewing breathtaking vistas of sloping tiled roofs mingling harmoniously with the trees, sky, and mountains, my legs ached, but my head throbbed from the overflow of information poured in by Mr. Kim. He laughed wildly at his own jokes between our history lessons. In museums, Mr. Kim recited the years of Korean dynasties as we marveled over exhibits of royal relics. To make sure we were listening, he shouted out surprise quizzes. "What year did Gyeong-ju become the capital of Shilla Dynasty?"

Donnie answered, "57 B.C."

"You get ten points!" Mr. Kim said. "What is national flower?"

Anxious to get points, I shouted, "Hibiscus?"

"Only two points for easy question," Mr. Kim said. *Okay, he's a male chauvinist.*

Like the Energizer bunny, Mr. Kim went on and on, exhausting me. Resting wearily in his van after our intensive tour, I dreamed of a hot bath and soft bed while Mr. Kim drove us to our Korean "home." While making plans from Minnesota, I told Donnie I'd like to stay in a traditional Korean home.

Careening around a sharp corner into an alley, Mr. Kim screeched to a halt. "This is nobleman's house." Staring at dying flowers and shrubs in the dry, cracked dirt beside the long, narrow path to the weathered one-story house, I found this hard to believe. I found this difficult to believe.

An ancient face framed with white hair peered out at us from a low window as we neared the simple bungalow. My heart sank as I realized she was sitting on the floor. This did not look good.

A slim Korean woman with black hair wearing a striped button-down shirt and brown trousers came out to greet us. "Welcome. My name Rose. I show you room."

I gasped out loud when a man looking exactly like the fierce-looking giant wooden temple guards Mr. Kim had called 'monsters' came out the door. Square and stocky, wild black hair with long bangs, big nose, and wide eyes established Mongolian ancestry. He gave me a menacing grin. My heart thumped.

Hoping the man wouldn't follow us, I stuck close to Rose as she led us into a separate building beside the house. "You sleep here," she said. I stopped short at the doorway, staring at the vast, empty room with ugly green walls. There wasn't a stick of furniture. "Where is the bed?" I cried.

"You sleep on mats."

Not wanting to hurt Rose's feelings, I reminded myself this was part of my Korean experience.

Rose turned to Donnie. "Your room in another building." She pointed to a building on the other side of her house.

Oh, no! Forget courtesy! "I'm too tired to sleep on the floor." I said, asking Mr. Kim to drive us to a hotel.

"No, you stay here tonight."

On the verge of crying, I insisted, "I can't! I need a bed and a bathtub! Please!"

Reluctantly, Mr. Kim agreed. I turned to leave, but looming in the doorway, the fierce-looking barbarian blocked our way. He growled, "Good room. You stay."

I staggered back, smashing into Mr. Kim. Pushing me away he said, "He say you cannot go. You stay here. That's the deal."

"I'm exhausted! I need a bed."

Mr. Kim shrugged. "He say you stay."

Rose ran across the room. "I show you. More mats." Opening a cupboard door set in the wall, she proudly pointed at shelves filled with folded mats. "You can have more mats. Two mats. Three mats."

Scanning the room again, I mentally ticked off the problems: No bed, no chair, no food, and no car. I pictured myself huddled on the mat all night, cold and scared, thinking about the "barbarian monster" lurking next door.

Seeing the tears pooling in my eyes, understanding my fear, Donnie put his arm around me and said, "I'll sleep in here too." Turning to Rose he said, "We'll both stay in here."

Smiling happily, she opened a small door next to the cupboard. "Bathroom."

There it was—a hole in the floor. "No! My knees are screaming, my legs wobbly from climbing steps, I can't squat. Donnie—I can't stay here!"

Donnie said, "We're going." Mercifully, Mr. Kim relented. As we went out the door, her husband glaring at us, I apologized profusely to Rose: "I'm sorry. I'm so sorry."

Mr. Kim drove us to The Tourist Hotel. Anxiously opening the door to the room, I yelled, "A real bed!" Green slippers at the doorway welcomed me. Rushing to the bathroom I yelled, "A real bathroom with a shower, and a "foreigner" toilet!" I flopped on the bed relishing the luxury!

The next morning, Mr. Kim icily ignored me. We visited palaces, temples, fifth century relics from an excavated tomb, and museums. We climbed up thousands of steps and clambered over treacherous rocks to temples carved in caves. At the last stop, I rebelled against climbing narrow, spiral stairs up to a Buddha overlooking the tree tops. Mr. Kim insisted, "You climb up to Buddha."

I finally shouted, "No. I will not climb up there. I'm not going to risk my life." Only the teenagers were climbing up, older Koreans weren't attempting the climb. "Look, they're not going up." Finally, Mr. Kim led us back down.

I was more than ready to take that bullet train back to Donnie's apartment in Seoul!

Chapter 29
Experiencing the Facilities

Touring through several countries on our Scandinavian tour, I had announced to Carol as I mopped up another bathroom, "I'm tired of cleaning bathrooms all through Europe."

Scanty shower curtains flapping open caused floods. Hand-held shower heads inevitably were pointed to flood the floor or to soak the one hand towel and one bath towel allotted per person. Showers without walls in small bathrooms, apparently added as an afterthought, could cause an electrifying experience; I cautiously reminded myself to wait until ankle-deep water was safely drained away before using the hair dryer. For short people (me) it required a high hurdle to step in and out of tubs with high, curved sides.

Ritzier European bathrooms had two luxuries not commonly found in American hotels: heated floors and heated towel racks. When I grabbed the hot towel rack to help pull myself out of the high tub, I yelped—it burnt my palm. High-class or not, European bathrooms are dangerous.

We learned several languages as we went from country to country. Well, maybe just the word for restrooms. Leaping out of the bus for our Norwegian tour guide's "tea and wee" stops, we frantically searched for signs reading Toilette, Toaletter, and other versions. Pictures on the doors helped us understand that Herrers must be his, not hers, because Dames are hers.

Integrated lines for unisex bathrooms become intimate when thirty-five people race off the bus. Men unzip and zip out quickly, then impatiently ask wives, "What took you so long?" They received lectures about ladies' lines. Some stalls had private little washbasins, which extended the waiting-in-line time. The bold overflowed into Men.

Often, we needed money to use a bathroom. We'd fumble with strange change from other countries, trying to find the correct coin needed for a slot on a door. Ladies courteously hold open the door for the next person, so turnstiles prevented more than one person using the same coin.

Eating lunch at the fashionable NK department store in Sweden, we watched women paying a guard at the door of the restroom. Between bites of Swedish almond cake, we scrambled through confusing coins from previous countries. A woman at the next table kindly offered to help, selecting five Kroner from our outstretched hands. Clutching my coins I marched up to the toilette guard. Stifling a smile she said, "You don't have to pay because you ate here." Apparently she enjoyed our comedy skit.

Solving the flushing problem was sometimes a puzzle. "What do you push?" would come floating out from the stalls. Some had a knob in the top of the tank to pull up, some knobs pushed down, and some were ingeniously hidden as part of the tank. Or they might be disguised on the wall or the floor. Regardless, they rarely had much flushing power. At the historic Palace Theatre we tried to hide our smirks as sophisticated women in elegant dresses queuing up at the loo during intermission yelled, "It won't flush." The stench was not as nasty as an outhouse in a hunting shack in the Minnesota woods, but still, offensive.

That first encounter with a Korean restroom in Incheon International Airport brought me to a halt. I stood staring at the small hole in the floor before quickly running out, hoping nobody saw me in the men's bathroom. But no, the picture on the door was a woman. Perplexed, I looked around. With a sigh of relief, I went into a door marked "Foreigner Toilette." As soon as I saw my brother, I asked, "Do you have a regular toilet?" Relieved that he did, I said. "You forgot to tell me to strengthen my legs for squatting."

Women's restrooms in the better restaurants in Seoul sometimes had fancy oval-shaped porcelain bowls depressed into the floor, prettily painted with flowers waiting to be watered. But when I walked into the restroom in Gyeong-ju I sagged in disbelief. Mr. Kim had taken us to a friend's small repair shop to wait for his other customers. Of course, I needed a bathroom.

I paced around a drain in the floor like a dog sniffing a fire hydrant, wondering if I could delay this pit stop. Urgency forced me to squat. I reminded myself that I'd used this method while snowmobiling, unbundling from a bulky, one-piece snowmobile suit to hunker down in the snow. I smiled to myself as I remembered the time my friend, co-worker and avid snowmobiler, Margaret, peed into her hood.

If you plan to go to South Korea, my advice is to train with leg weights to strengthen your leg muscles. And if you'd like to experience a bed and breakfast in a Korean home, don't do any sightseeing that would exhaust you—save your energy.

I still giggle as I remember the shock of seeing a man with a roll of toilet paper in his hand guarding two stalls in a tiny underground rest stop. That round Portuguese entrepreneur in a black beret is engraved in my mind.

Back home in Minnesota, I'm overjoyed to use my own bathroom again. Oh, except for the catastrophe with Maax.

Chapter 30
Maax and Me
Dove Island 2010

I'm having a conference with two men in my bathroom, swearing them to secrecy. "Don't tell Leo!"

Last night, while Leo was watching TV downstairs, I was upstairs battling with Maax, my newly installed tub. It sprouted a tsunami, morphing into a watery volcano that nearly drowned me before flooding the bathroom.

Yesterday, Chuck chopped out the old mauve tub and plumbed in the new bone-white Jacuzzi, and an electrician, Mickey, wired it. Excited for my first bath, I stopped to read directions. Under instructions on "How to operate the electronic controls for the Hydromax and Aerofeel systems," the manual coached, "touch the symbols—one to set the timer, another to turn on the pumps, and a third to turn on the blower for hydrotherapy." A big problem—I couldn't find any symbols. My old Jacuzzi had a simple timer, I set it for ten minutes, it dinged, and I was done, just like cooking in the microwave.

Giving up on operating systems, I thumbed through the manual for information about the water level—I've had problems before with too much water in a Jacuzzi. Finding nothing, I threw down the manual. Giggling about a simple bath becoming so complex, I turned on the hot water and poured in lavender bubble bath for an old-fashioned jetless bath. Settled in the tub, a light flashed on the oval panel with the Maax label. I punched it, another symbol lit up—and the jets roared to life. Stretching out, I closed my eyes for a relaxing bath. Suddenly, water covered my face and I fought my way up. Swirling and bubbling, the water rose higher and higher until soapy waves were splashing out of the tub onto the floor. *Oops.* Too much water in the tub.

Fighting through bubbles and spraying water, I scrambled out of the tub and grabbed the manual with shaky hands, searching for instructions on how to turn off this monster. Finally: "The system starts or stops with the pump symbol." Climbing back in, fighting bubbles and water still gushing over the symbols and out of the tub, I blindly jabbed my finger at the panel until the jets stopped.

Dragging myself out of the tub again, I dumped all the towels out of the linen closet and crawled on the floor mopping up bubbles and water. My heart lurched when I saw water flowing around the motors. Thankful that Leo had made the wise decision not to build a wood enclosure until we'd tested the tub, I hid the wet towels in my laundry basket and made sure I didn't leave any watery evidence on the floor.

With trembling legs, clinging to the railing, I walked downstairs in my fuzzy pink bathrobe. Nothing like a bath to turn a person into an absolute wreck. The new tub is named Sincerity and I'm sincerely sorry I bought it. Leo asked, "How was the tub?"

I muttered, "You won't like it." He didn't use the jets, but liked our former mauve tub because it was spacious enough to sprawl out and every now and then sneak a pre-sleep nap with his bath. "Maax is smaller." I didn't mention I might have broken it.

After a sleepless night, I tested the tub. On the verge of tears, I called Chuck and confessed I'd ruined the motor with a flood. Pacing the floor until he and Mickey arrived, I almost collapsed in tears of relief when Mickey soothingly said it was only a blown breaker. Maax wasn't broken!

How many people does it take to figure out how to take a bath? Only three— plumber, electrician and me.

That night I had the pleasure of a relaxing bath with jets—and no flood.

Chapter 31
Bailey Goes to Texas
Co-Author—Bailey (Bichon Frise) Karsnia

Yay! Yay! I'm on my way! I'm on my way to Texas. I don't like staying behind when my family travels far and wide. One day while taking a pre-dinner nap on the couch, I perked up my ears. Just what I feared, Mom and Dad are spelling T.R.I.P. I'm only a little white Bichon Frise but I'm a smartie.

Whenever they go away, they make me stay at their daughter Sherry's place. With a grin on my face I remember how Sherry and her husband, Jim, scolded "Bad dog," when I played bad tricks. Sherry yelled lots when she stepped in my wet spots. A hunger strike worked great; I'd sniff my food and walk away until they bought me steak.

But life for me wasn't so great when their daughter Jenna married Luke and they adopted a golden retriever puppy, Casey. Casey became a bouncing pain. Life got worse when a baby came! Everyone fussed over Nissa Marie and forgot about me. My life isn't carefree when Nissa Marie torments me, crawling, grabbing my tail—oweeee! I'm being abuuused!

I love living on Rainy Lake with Mom and Dad, boat rides are great. I sit on the dock staring at the boat, begging for a ride. But I get a long face on Sundays with family at our place and Casey eats off my plate.

Now I'm banned from Sherry's for being bad, but I'm not sad. I deserve to go on vacation because I'm a working dog. Every day: *Hi ho, hi ho, it's off to work I go.* At Leo's Sawmill I'm top office dog, watching Dad as he saws, barking when customers come. I'm security guard, too, sniffing the paths, searching for trespassers.

Today, as we drive away from the lake, silently I wait until we're way past Sherry's place. Then up I pop! A happy little dog because I'm going along. In the back seat of the truck I snuggle in my blue bed, jumping up now and then to check where we're going, where we've been. In front on the wide console between Mom and Dad, I take a few licks of water from my cup in the holder, then back to nap. *Life is good.*

We left International Falls in a snowstorm, but Iowa, Missouri, and Kansas are brown. Nights, we stop where Comfort Inns allow pets and I sleep on a bed. Help! At Round Rock Comfort Inn Mom came out to say, "No pets allowed." I'm stuck sleeping in the truck. Burrowing in my cozy bed I try to be brave.

RRRRRumble! Lightning flashes! Boom! Thunder crashes. How I hate thunderstorms! At home, I leap up into the bed and snuggle between Dad's legs. Tonight, no howling for help. No yelping help! I tremble and whine until the storm stops. Finally my eyes close and I doze. In the morning, Mom and Dad praise me for being brave.

On the ferry to Port Aransas, we watch sailboats and seagulls swoop. Bounding through the door at their son Al's yellow house I stop short. Yikes! Another crawler! We stare eye-to-eye. Same name as me, Bailey Lee, crawls up to me, shouts with glee, grabs my tail or my ears. EEEEow! I hide under my blankee but Bailey Lee won't leave. She squats, watching me. What relief to escape upstairs to a peaceful place where Mom and Dad sleep. Nobody's there to torment me.

Next day—I get a surprise! Our Minnesota family arrives eager to celebrate Easter, all eighteen together. My buddy, thirteen-year-old Tyler, covers me with hugs and kisses. Nissa toddles in, spots me. She stops, begs: "Where's Casey, Where's Casey?" Wild Casey didn't get to come. I'm feeling smug—I got to come! I stay alert so I don't get hurt. Two babies in hot pursuit: a walker and a crawler, two surprising speedsters. I scamper as fast as I can to stay out of reach.

Spring breakers and families are spread for miles and miles on the beach, in motor homes and tents, sunning in chairs or on blankets. Dogs large and small pull at leashes, straining to make friends with me. Strutting by with my family I ignore their barking. I have responsibilities, my family needs watching: Bailey Lee crawling fast across the sand, Nissa gasping in waves, Jackie and Tyler on a board, skimming and falling. Oops! Adam tumbles head over heels.

All too soon, my Minnesota family is packing, loading cars, kissing and hugging. Three carloads leave, driving away and waving. Suddenly, I feel lonely and sad, would be glad to dash from getting my tail grabbed. But walking on the beach without noisy spring breakers was a treat. Dad and I take early morning walks on the warm sand. Seagulls and pelicans dive over rolling, crashing waves.

After a few blissful days, Mom and Dad are packing. What are they thinking? Don't they remember leaving home with snow falling? Retracing our drive through many states we're soon back to Minnesota cold. Pulling into our driveway, Dad said, "Bailey, you were so good on this long ride." I fluff up with pride.

Walking on a sandy beach instead of snowy concrete was a special treat I'd like to repeat. Living in the "Ice Box of the Nation" in northern Minnesota, spring arrives slooowly.

Spring Struggles

Spring struggles for birth;
Winter tenaciously clings;
Spring sloshes through snow.

Chapter 32
Quebec Quest
2005

C'est magnifique I breathe as Donnie and I walk past grand nineteenth-century buildings on the tree-lined cobblestoned streets of Montreal. I'm back in Paris—for a moment, anyway. The suitcase bumping along behind me returns me to reality. I'm trudging from the bus station to the Taj Mahal with my brother—the Taj Mahal in Montreal, Quebec, not India. Quebec's Taj Mahal is a seedy hotel that my budget-minded sibling has booked for our one night in this glorious city, chosen as much for price as its proximity to bus and train stations.

There's no elevator. Dragging my suitcase up four flights, thumping down again the next morning, along sidewalks, up ramps, down more steps, and finally reaching the train, I slumped into my seat, exhausted.

Pastoral scenes of pine trees and fields of corn, farm homes and barns, whizzed past our windows. The rhythm of humming tracks, buzzing conversations, and wailing train whistle lulled me into a half sleep, inspiring a poem:

> Backpacking, backpacking
> Whose idea was that?
> Although the pack
> Is not on my back
> But pulled on rollers behind
> On Montreal city sidewalks wide,
> Up and down hotel steps
> Down and up subway steps.
> On board Via Rail train
> Train whistle wails.
> Past open fields and plains.
> Dozens of conversations buzz
> Train tracks hum.

The taxi driver slammed on his brakes when Donnie gave him the address for our next economy hotel. "Too far out of city, you should take a bus." Quickly, I asked, "Is there a good hotel close by?" A U-turn on a dime and we were whisked to a hotel with a canopy emblazoned with Loews LeConcorde. Before we were out of the car, our bags were unloaded and in the hands of a bellboy. I negotiated with the desk clerk about the price of the rooms; she'd disappear to check with the manager, returning with a new price. At the final offer, looking at Donnie hopefully, when he nodded I mouthed "thank you." Donnie doesn't question prices for gourmet dining, but dislikes paying for pricey hotel rooms. I love sumptuous surroundings, but scrimping on food doesn't bother me. Could we compromise?!

Grinning with delight at the room, I gratefully tipped the bellboy when he carried my luggage to room 605. Two big beds, fluffy white towels hanging in an ornate bathroom with black marble countertop, gold faucets, and large mirror framed in gold assuaged my disgust with the Taj Mahal.

At the concierge's suggestion, we went on a self-guided walking tour. Going through St. Jean's gate, part of the ancient wall that protected the city in an earlier century, we admired European style buildings with fancy gable roofs, dormers, and window boxes overflowing with flowers. On the promenade along the St. Lawrence River, I looked up at the Frontenac Chateau, its turrets and green roof towering over the square, a copy of a chateau in France. Formerly owned by the Canadian Pacific Railway, it was designed by the architect Bruce Price, a member of the wealthy Price family who owned a paper mill in Quebec. (Working at Boise Paper for many years, I'm interested in paper mills.)

Ancestors of our St. Pierre and Martell grandparents began coming to the Quebec area in the 1600 and 1700s. Aunt Cecelia was enthusiastic about our genealogy. "I'm named after Cecelia, an ancestor who was one of the '"King's Daughters.'" I hated to disillusion my aunt, but my research revealed we are not of royal blood. In 1663 the King recruited hundreds of "filles des marier," young women in poverty but of good quality. He promised them a dowry if they went to New France, hoping they would marry soldiers and men of property to populate his new colony. Considering the number of descendants in our family tree, they did a fine job of populating!

A savory cheese omelet and lean Canadian bacon in the lovely hotel dining room didn't prepare me for our nerve-racking day. First, the concierge made many phone calls to car rental agencies before finding one available car at the railroad station. When we rented the red Pontiac Sunfire from Sandor, I gave up trying to understand his French-English directions to Pont Pierre la Ponte Bridge, the longest non-tolled suspension bridge in the world, the bridge over St. Lawrence River that would take us to the Trans-Canada Highway. Because I'm directionally challenged, I offered to drive so Donnie could navigate.

"Oops! We should have turned there," Donnie said. More directions, more miles, more circling made me discouraged. "Let's take the car back and forget the whole trip!"

Donnie calmly said, "It doesn't matter. I don't get upset because my decisions are inconsequential. God's decisions are important." He took over as driver and I relaxed.

Laughing when Pont Pierre la Ponte Bridge finally loomed in front of us, Donnie said, "Nobody would believe we couldn't find the largest suspension bridge in the country." (Well, yes, my family would.) On Route 20, we screeched to a halt when we saw the sign, "St. Pierre." Finding the cemetery quickly in that small village, we tramped up and down peering at graves, but found no St. Pierre tombstones. At the small store—the only store—the teenage clerk shrugged that she had no idea how the village got its name; neither did the two young customers buying beer. Oh, well, we felt famous as we posed with the St. Pierre sign.

After fortifying ourselves with sandwiches in the town of Montmagny, I felt brave enough to drive again. The Auto Road was posted 60-100, but with my speedometer at 100, cars whizzed past like we were standing still. With sweaty hands and white knuckles, I desperately tried to keep the Pontiac in my lane as gusts of wind tossed the small car around like a toy.

In the late afternoon, we stopped in Kamouraska at AuRelaise Restaurant. We hit the jackpot! Between gourmet courses, I dashed outside to devour one of Kamouraska's famous sunsets, capturing photos of glorious clouds and sky sweeping between the river and heavenly horizon.

Driving along St. Lawrence River, we were treated to an explosion of changing colors, pastels of lavender and cotton candy pink turning to brilliant red. Gazing spellbound at the sky, I dreamily envisioned God painting waves of colors on his blue canvas. Our joy lasted many miles before the dazzling sunset left us with a sense of loss and a dark night of driving.

I exclaimed, "No wonder our ancestors settled here. Petit St. Pierre and Judith Milville-Deschenes were married in Ste-Anne-de-la-Pocatiere in Kamouraska in 1758. Our grandfather, Alfred St. Pierre, is a direct descendant of the St. Pierre's who lived in Kamouraska. I wonder why he left."

Donnie didn't stop until 11:00 p.m. I may have been a bit grumpy by the time he pulled up at Rimouski Hotel. The hotel clerk said, "We're completely filled. There isn't a single bed in all of Rimouski. Hotels are filled from here to Quebec."

I wailed, "Oh, no. We came from Quebec."

She said, "All you can do is keep going and hope you find a motel." With a sinking heart, I trudged out with the bad news. Although it was pitch black, traffic was thick. Donnie was driving 90 on a winding road and cars were passing us. Gripping the door handle tightly, trying to brake from my side, I searched the blackness for a motel that wasn't flashing No Vacancy.

Miles raced by before I saw car lights turning into a motel "Stop! There's a motel with a vacancy sign." Donnie turned the car around and I raced into the office. A woman, looking as exhausted as I felt, was signing for a room. The owner said, "Only one room left."

Normally I don't like old motels, but I was desperate. "Does it have two beds?"

With a French accent, the man replied, "Yes, two beds. You want to see it?"

"No. I'll take it." I had to get out of the car. The little cabin with blonde faux-paneled walls apparently had been decorated in the 1950s. Sailboats were painted on the headboards of the twin beds; the homemade floral bedspreads edged with ruffles were faded. Staring down at the wavy stripes of orange, red, green and brown carpet, I told Donnie, "I wouldn't want to come in here drunk. It makes me nauseous as it is." A small broken TV sat on top of a blue painted desk. However, the bed was comfortable and I slept well.

Donnie showered first in the morning, and then went to the motel office/dining room for breakfast. In the shower, I chastised myself for laughing at the little cabin; the white ceiling and walls were scrupulously clean.

Donnie burst through the door. "You missed a lively breakfast. A man wearing a black studded belt like a carpenter's tool belt with three harmonicas in the pockets played O'Susanna and other tunes. There were some couples and a family of four. They were all chatting and laughing, kissing and hugging, and when anyone left, he'd play *Olde Lang Syne*.

I hurried over, but only one couple was left. Waiting for my toast to pop up, trying to read the labels of several jars of jam, I pointed and asked the owner, "You made?" She stopped clearing dishes off the tables and found a dictionary, then translated the names of the berry jams. I sampled the delicious black currant.

Driving along the St. Lawrence River on Highway 132, old-fashioned rural homes and beautiful lake homes showcased masses of flowers. In several cemeteries, we found a plethora of names on our "tree." Feeling so excited about people who died long ago, I began to wish we could find some who were still alive.

Donnie caught a glimpse of a sign on a garage with a family name from our genealogy chart—Gagnon Alignment and Balance. Our father, with only an eighth grade education, owned Phil's Garage, a small repair shop with the only alignment machine in town. When he had his own car dealership, he sold other brands but he named his garage St. Pierre Buick because Buicks were his favorite. My favorite too! If our dad had inherited his mechanical ability, it had skipped Donnie and me—along with a sense of direction.

Gentilleries Creperie's served a perfect Sunday lunch, savory crepes filled with asparagus and broccoli, accompanied by sides of fruit and tasty potato slices. While waiting for our crepes, I strolled around the dining room looking at pictures of pioneer families on the walls. "Look, Donnie, this picture of George Pelletier resembles you and Daddy." (Writing this, I'm wondering why we didn't ask about him.)

Contented from our crepes breakfast, we drove past waves of purple and gold wildflowers swaying in the breeze, creating a mosaic worthy of a Monet painting. People in villages were relaxing in the sunshine on porches attached to well-maintained homes with turrets, dormers, and balconies. In rural areas, farm houses were surrounded by green fields and huge silos. The daytime panoramic scene of blue horizon over the St. Lawrence coastline was almost as breathtaking as the awesome sunset from last night.

Reminiscing, I told Donnie, "I think I'm communing with the spirits of our French ancestors who settled here. The owner of our motel reminded me of Grandma Dina St. Pierre. Grandma died before you were born, but I remember her. Grandpa Alfred was only forty-eight years old when he died of a heart attack, and Grandma took in washing and ironing to earn a living. Aunt Alice told me she had to deliver the clean, ironed laundry with a red wagon, and she hated it, but sometimes she got a nickel tip. Grandma always had a kettle of soup bubbling on the wood stove and homemade bread from the oven. Despite working hard, Grandma enjoyed life. I remember her playing cards at the round oak table in her dining room, laughing and shouting in French."

This time, the monstrous Pont Pierre la Ponte Bridge didn't play hide and seek. At Normandie's, a large, cafeteria type restaurant, we had communication problems with our scowling waitress. After our gourmet meals in Kamorouska, I could barely choke down the dry chicken sandwich on stale white bread, but a customer gave us good directions to the rail station. When we parked the Pontiac I didn't even say good-bye, I was so happy to be out of it.

Donnie made a hotel reservation from the station before hailing a cab. At Fleur De Lys (happily, a fine hotel in the heart of old Quebec) I washed away my aches and pains in a hot bath, and a seven-hour sleep revived me enough to bound out of bed on Monday morning for a countryside tour to Ile d'Orleans.

We walked down a very long staircase for breakfast in a coffee café. Quebec City has lots of hills, with twenty-nine outdoor public staircases, supposedly to make it easier to get around. It was a steep climb back up in the heat to wait for a tour bus.

Joe, the bus driver, who looked like a permanent resident on the island, provided historical tidbits. "The statue of Samuel de Champlain honors him for founding Quebec City in 1608 after persuading Henry IV to let him set up a colony in 'New France.' Ile d'Orleans is an island just outside Quebec with six unique parishes, and a large percentage of French Canadians trace their ancestry to the early residents. It's surrounded by the Laurentian and Appalachian Mountains. The first settlers came in 1650 and by 1750, there were six thousand people living in New France. Now there are ninth and tenth generations living on the island. The current population of seven thousand swells to twenty-four thousand in summer.

"The island is self-sufficient with industries related to farming, water, forests, hunting or logging. Fur trade was phenomenal in the 1800s. The Price family lived here while making their money in the timber industry, and today a skyscraper in Quebec houses their headquarters. (We saw it, remember?) There are lots of millionaires on the island, plus billionaire farmers raising Appaloosa horses."

There were interesting stops and shops. Chocolaterie de Ile d'Orleans, a charming shop, sold delicious chocolate. At the Albert Gilles Museum, known for copper art, the artist's daughter said that her father decorated many homes and public buildings, among them GM and Chrysler, and the homes of Walt Disney and Mae West. Proudly showing us an astounding work of art, fifty glittering gold panels depicting the life of Christ, she said, "My father spent fifteen years creating Christorama." At Chez Marie fresh bread baking in the wood stove permeated all corners of the little stone house. Marie, the fourth generation running the shop, bakes fifty loaves of bread every day. For one dollar, Marie offered a thick slice of warm bread slathered with real Maple syrup. One was not enough!

Did you know that Niagara Falls isn't as high as Quebec's Montmorency Falls? Montmorency is the highest falls in Quebec, ninety feet higher than Niagara Falls, and plunges over a high cliff into the St. Lawrence River. After negotiating a scary suspension bridge that swayed with each step, we walked down staircases winding around the roaring waterfalls, giving us stunning views from various angles.

At Sainte-Anne-de-Beaupre, a pilgrimage site dedicated to Jesus' Grandmother Anne, three priests were conducting a mass. Every year, over a million people visit the sanctuary. Elegant panels on the walls were painted in France in 1884. In Rome I loved the church honoring Jesus' mother; now, I feel a sense of peace in this church honoring His grandmother.

After saying Bonjour to Sainte Anne's Church and the charming island, it seemed appropriate to have lunch at Saint Anne's Restaurant. An outside table under a canopy, a gentle breeze, a sidewalk musician playing a guitar and singing, and an eclectic parade of people to watch—life is good.

We made the difficult climb back up the steep steps to Fleur de Lys to collect our luggage. Luckily, a new guest arrived at the hotelier and we snared the taxi for our trip to the train station, where they weighed our bags before loading them. "I've been hauling around thirty-two pounds, no wonder I get tired!"

Unsympathetically, Donnie responded, "You should have packed lighter."

The motion of the train, the clickety clack of the tracks, and the haunting sound of the whistle lulled me into a delicious nap before arriving back in Montreal. Good thing, too, because I had to pull my suitcase down the street to the Europeen Hotel, just as bad as its neighbor, Montreal's slum Taj Mahal. Wearily, I dragged my thirty-two pound suitcase up ten steps into the office and then up to second floor. At least it's only one night, I consoled myself as we savored spicy manicotti at The Italian Restaurant.

Donnie's phone call woke me. "Our tour bus will be picking us up at 9:15. Our room includes a continental breakfast to bring to our room." A few minutes later, my considerate brother tapped at the door with a tray of coffee, orange juice, and muffins.

While waiting for our tour bus, a garbage truck pulled up and provided entertainment. Music blaring from across the street apparently inspired the garbage man to perform an impromptu ballet, twirling black bags of trash into the open jaws of the truck. Who'd ever believe that tossing garbage could develop into an impressive dance?

Nearly everyone got off the double-decker bus at Plaza Marie where there are thirty-two miles of underground shopping and fifteen hundred shops. Donnie and I continued riding to Notre Dame Basilica. Celene Dion was married in the Sacred Chapel and her baby was baptized there. One hundred weddings are performed in the Sacred Chapel each year. The guide joked, "There's a two and one-half year wait. If you break up, keep your reservation. You still have time to find a new partner."

Other places of interest: The second oldest house in Montreal, Chateau Ranezoly, was built in 1705 for the Governor of Montreal, the fourteenth governor who had fourteen children. (I wonder if he did it on purpose.) The tallest skyscraper is fifty-one stories high, and has a triangular top. We also learned that the first industry in Montreal was trading, the second industry wood, and today it's farming and education.

"In 2009, Montreal was named North America's number one host city for international association events," our guide bragged. "The theme of Expo 67 was 'Man and His World' and they built concrete cube condos called Habitat 67, designed as modern homes in crowded cities." I thought they looked ugly but our guide said, "Only millionaires can afford to live in the condos; they're built so they can have private yards with flowers and neighbors can't see in windows.

"A big stadium built for the 1976 Olympics is nicknamed 'The Big O,' a reference to both its name and to the doughnut shape of the stadium's roof." Almost snickering, he added, "A second nickname is 'The Big Owe' because of the astronomical cost of the stadium. See the leaning tower they put at the base of the stadium? This 'quirky' building is called the Montreal Tower and is the tallest inclined tower in the world." I wondered if they should be proud of the "Big O." To me, that inclined tower looks like it's inclined to fall on top of the "Big Owe."

On our way to Montreal Airport to fly to New York City, our Lebanese cab driver told me he came here in 1990. "I already knew French because it's the second language in Lebanon," he said, "and I made up my mind to learn English also." He really impressed me, an immigrant owning his own cab and knowing three languages. I scolded myself for not learning a second language.

At the Montreal Airport, the customs officer looked at my passport and asked, "Do you know Mondale?" Startled, I said, "Well, I know he was a former Minnesota governor."

He said, "I worked for him and when he went fishing in International Falls, I went too." I asked, "Did you catch fish?" He replied, "No, that wasn't my job. That was the governor's job." Fishing is a job? Tell that to the fishing widows when the fishing opener begins on Mother's Day!

Chapter 33
NYC Theater Blast
2005 continued

New York City is approximately five hundred miles from Quebec. Donnie talked me into a little side trip to see Broadway shows, plays he carefully chose before leaving Korea.

Fighting crowds and smoke, we found Walter Kerr Theatre. After standing in line to buy tickets for *Doubt*, we joined another line to go inside the theater. Already, I was sick of lines. Donnie and I didn't have seats together, but my seat was excellent. *Doubt* cast doubt on the Irish priest who may or may not have molested a twelve-year-old black boy. The mother of the molested child does not want to rock the boat because his father was violent and they needed the priest's. kindness and special attention. The young teacher didn't believe the priest was guilty. It was a real cliffhanger when the principal surprised the audience by revealing her own doubt.

At the Primitivo Restaurant, while enjoying Ravioli alla Vodka, we reviewed the play Donnie tested me. "What was the priest's sermon about in the first scene?"

I said, "His metaphor was about a shipwrecked sailor who found debris to float on, setting his course for home by the star. Clouds came, covering the stars. The sailor was beset by doubt—should he stay the course or not? I mulled over the play, trying to decide for myself if the priest was guilty. Reluctantly, I settled on the guilty verdict.

Returning to Nederlander Theatre for the evening play, *Rent*, we were thrilled with our excellent seats in the fifth row of the Mezzanine. *Rent*, with a stark setting of a low-rent tenement district and minimal set changes, offered a provocative essay on today's culture. The actors not only had superb voices, they were agile, jumping on and off tables and chairs; my legs and knees hurt just from watching them. Engrossed in the lives of these people battling poverty, addictions, prostitution, and diseases, I cried when Angel died of AIDS and Mimi nearly died.

Tammy, an old school chum, insisted we had to stay at her apartment because "New York hotels are too expensive," generously arranging to sleep at a friend's. She'd assured me that every cab driver knew how to find Thirteenth Street in Greenwich Village, "it's a landmark street." Ours did not! However, while cruising down Thirteenth Street, I recognized the red door to her apartment building. Pulling my thirty-two pound suitcase up to the third floor on the narrow, winding staircase, I stood panting until Tammy opened her door and welcomed us with hugs.

Her charming apartment has a fireplace, an eclectic array of furniture, and, my favorite, a picture of herself looking like Audrey Hepburn's twin. Pleased that we'd enjoyed the plays, she chatted with us, leaving at midnight to stay with her friend, Penelope. A full moon glistened outside her window; I drifted off to sleep, content that Tammy could see a slice of nature from her city window.

Tammy loves New York City. She moved there because she loves acting and wanted to become an actress. Houses on her street cost over one million dollars, but she's grandfathered in at the same rent as when she moved there at age nineteen. She's gotten small roles in plays, and loves her part-time job at the Metropolitan Museum of Art, meeting famous actors and celebrities.

Tammy wants me to love New York City. I try. New York City zaps my energy. Waking up in Tammy's twin bed to the sound of garbage trucks banging, sirens wailing, traffic roaring, horns blaring, I compare it to waking up at home on Rainy Lake listening to the cry of a loon or a seagull. Maybe I'm homesick.

I'm overwhelmed with New York's crowded sidewalks, fighting for a seat on crowded subways, holding tightly to a strap, swaying and staggering when the subway train starts and stops. Wherever we went, Tammy would vanish, asking directions in the subway, on the street, and in stores. Looking around, we'd ask, "Where is she now?" She'd come out of a store smiling, "I meet lots of people when I ask directions."

Tammy took us to Ground Zero, saying, "I loved looking at the twin towers from my apartment. I nearly cry every time I look out at the empty hole. On 9/11, my block was roped off, and I had to show ID to get back to my apartment. Now, that empty space is a reminder of that terrible day." Being there, the terror came alive again. Seeing the photos, reading the pleas, recalling people fleeing for their lives, the panic that enveloped our entire country all came flooding back.

Climbing the wide marble steps into the Metropolitan Museum of Art, we stopped in surprise at the signs posted with prices for admission. Tammy had promised, "There's no admission, as little as fifty cents will admit you into 'my' museum." Donnie immediately paid fifteen dollars and took off. Overwhelmed, I wandered around studying posters, trying to decide what exhibits to see.

A guard made me buy a ticket before I could use the restroom. Then, charging into high gear, I toured Asia, China, Korea, medieval times, and the history of slavery. I was overjoyed at finding Egypt! I gazed on faces of mummies and the Sphinx, peered into tombs of ancient kings. Lost in far-away places, unaware of time, we rushed to catch a cab for New Amsterdam Theater, worried about being late for *Lion King*.

Theater enthusiast Tammy hadn't seen *Lion King*, so Donnie and I were thrilled to treat her to the play. There aren't enough adjectives to describe the spectacular *Lion King*. There was no attempt to hide the fact that people played the parts, but as the animals of the jungle poured onto the stage there were audible gasps at the spectacular creativity of the costumes. The two children playing young Simba and young Nala were amazing, acting, dancing and singing flawlessly. Captivated from beginning to end, I wondered how the performers kept their enthusiasm and energy night after night.

Still spellbound by the play, we followed Tammy to her favorite ice cream shop in Greenwich Village. Although he was ready to close, Derek greeted Tammy warmly, apologizing that he'd had such a busy night he didn't have all the flavors. Who cares? "Chocolate, please."

It was raining the next morning when we went to the Strand Bookstore on Broadway; the three-dollar umbrella I bought on a street corner was useless. Inside, we stood dripping rain and gawking at eighteen miles of books before splitting up to browse. Donnie bought books for friends, and I bought Maya Angelou's *Singin' and Swingin'* and *The Secret Life of Bees*. The *Bees* buzzed with me all the way home.

Dropping off our book purchases at the apartment, we walked to the restaurant Tea and Sympathy to meet Tammy. Asking a waitress for a table for three, she retorted, "I cannot seat you until the other person is here. Wait on that bench outside." With only a few tables crammed into a small space and one empty table, we understood.

When diners came out several minutes later, we went back in. Hustling by with a pot of coffee, the waitress sent us slinking back out to the bench. Brooding about how hungry I was for five minutes, I jumped up from the bench and said, "We haven't eaten anything today, my stomach is grumbling." As I pushed through the door, the waitress screamed, "You have to wait for the rest of your party."

I shouted back, "We're not waiting any longer. We're eating without her."

Scowling, the waitress seated us at a table with two chairs. Sampling their scrumptious sandwiches, I said, "I guess they have a right to be snooty." Tammy, who knew better than to try joining us, waited on the bench outside to escort us to our next play.

I was upset with *Glen Garry Glen Ross*. I hated the plot: an office of dishonest salesmen, swearing and scheming against each other. However, my brother—the drama teacher—said the acting was superb. Alan Alda has a great stage presence." Later, I admitted the acting had been good, but, call me a prude, the swearing and scheming upset me too much to enjoy the play.

Tammy insisted on accompanying us to the Museum of Modern Art (MoMA). "I can get you in free; it's another benefit from my job at Metropolitan Museum." When the subway train stopped, Donnie and I rushed inside. From out seats, we stared open-mouthed when we saw Tammy, still outside, running to another door. Before the doors closed, we heard her ask, "Is this the right train to . . . ?" The doors closed. Donnie and I watched her mouthing "I'll see you at the museum" as we sped past. Looking at Donnie in panic, I said, "But we don't know where to get off."

Hanging on to backs of seats I stumbled over to the man she'd asked for directions. "That was our guide. Where do we get off for the Museum of Modern Art?" He mumbled, "I don't know." Shuffling back to my seat, crestfallen, I whined, "What do we do now?" Suddenly, the man stood in front of us, asking "Did you mean MoMA?" We nodded. "You can get off anywhere from Forty-seventh to Fiftieth Street." At Forth-seventh, we waited on a bench, eyes peeled for Tammy. We chased after her when she got off at Fiftieth.

Crowds prevented us from seeing the special exhibit of Cezanne and Picasso that Donnie wanted to see, so he went to study Paintings and

Sculpture while I found an impressive photographic exhibit hoping to learn more about photography. I learned I had a lot to learn.

Returning from MoMA, Donnie and I finished last-minute packing while Tammy packed lunches for us. Donnie and I hugged good-bye and went to our separate gates: his to San Francisco, Tokyo, and South Korea. Although sad to see him leave, I was secretly happy I didn't have such a long flight to International Falls.

I marched around my seat for three hours vigilantly watching my luggage while times of departures were changed on the screen. Finally, the loud speaker announced that the plane was delayed. I was starved and I used the food voucher they gave me for a Whopper that tasted as good as any gourmet burger.

Of course, by the time my late plane landed at the Hubert H. Humphrey Airport in Minneapolis, the plane to International Falls had left. I received a voucher for a hotel room and a boarding pass for a morning flight. At the shuttle bus to the hotel, a woman handed me two more vouchers. "One is for the shuttle bus right now and one for morning." She cautioned, "Call this phone number tonight to make a reservation or you'll be left stranded in the morning,"

I was surprised to be taken to a Holiday Inn in St. Paul instead of one close to the airport. Leo sat at the Falls airport for two hours waiting for a plane I wasn't on. Before crawling into bed at 2:00 a.m. I left a wake-up call for 6:30, but the call was late. The shuttle driver said, "You're lucky I haven't left yet. You would have been stranded here."

Relieved to be at the airport, I stopped at a kiosk for coffee. The Pakistani lady wrapped in black kindly said, "I can't give you change. Buy something else, too." Thanking her for her suggestion, I bought a sandwich, coffee, and a bottle of water—and a good thing I did.

We boarded the plane for International Falls, and waited. We boarded another plane, and waited. Finally the pilot announced, "The left engine won't ignite and the mechanics went to get parts. It's minor, but we can't let you get off the plane until it's fixed." It didn't sound minor to me, but what was I to do besides pray? Leo had been told the plane would be on time and waited another two hours at the airport—but this time I did arrive, running to him for a comforting hug!

New York City, a fun place to visit, but it's heart breaking to see homeless people curled on concrete beds without pillows or blankets. Power-walking on the bike trail near my home, I see deer peeking out of the woods, watching me. Taking deep breaths of fresh air, I'm grateful I can enjoy a simple life, away from the crowds and smells and noise. The lake offers serenity. God knew what he was doing, keeping me in my home town while Tammy left to taste the Big Apple. Although, on her last visit here, Tammy said, "It's so beautiful. Why am I living in New York?"

UP NORTH HOMECOMING

Up north, traffic is lighter, pine forests thicker,
glimpses of lake instead of skyscrapers.

Dropping bags and baggage helter skelter
we wander gardens admiring new flowers.

Down at the dock, loons dance on the lake,
disappearing with lingering wail.

Squawking seagulls circle and swoop,
vigorously diving for food.

A mother duck proudly leads
a peaceful parade of fuzzy ducklings.

Breathing deep the clean breeze,
Savoring simple solitude serene . . .

Chapter 34
A Working Mother's Journey
Five decades later the glass ceiling is barely cracked
1963—2014

Working conditions have changed since 1963 when I was thrilled with a beat-up desk and a typewriter that needed pounding. Five decades later, sleek cubicles and computers replace them. We've made fantastic technological advances. Have working women made fantastic advances?

During my progression from typewriter to computer I faced the struggle of working mothers. Fifty years ago, women's monthly magazines raged that we were counterculture: "A mother's place is in the home." The seven years I worked as a nurse were acceptable—apparently nursing was considered an extension of nurturing. Taking an office job, I discovered a change in attitude and endured harassment from female co-workers.

Displeased Catholic in-laws equated working mothers with mortal sin. A few years ago, a sister-in-law commented, "Phyllis, I have to admit that your kids turned out well in spite of your working. But don't you wish you hadn't worked?"

"No," I said. "But I wish I'd hired a housekeeper."

Five decades later, sometimes the media quotes surveys that prove children are damaged by working mothers, other surveys prove children are damaged by non-working mothers. As the pendulum swings back and forth, it's the wrong choice no matter what.

Women are plagued by the same problems now that I faced in the 60s and feminist icon Gloria Steinem wrote about in the 80s. I remember the uproar when Barbara Walters (a woman!) signed a contract for a million dollars. An interesting chapter in her memoir, *Audition,* is titled, "Don't let the bastards get you down." She discloses gender inequity, harassment, and pay inequity in the 70s.

A distinct division of labor existed between married couples in the twentieth century. Husbands seldom did housework. Feeling "lucky" to be earning a salary, I raced home each day to become Super Woman, following my mother's rigid housework schedule.

In this new century, are parents sharing responsibilities? Apparently working women are still responsible for the lion's share of household responsibilities and child-raising. Today, women are asking questions: "Who is constructing glass ceilings? Is it the men at home or at the office? If men helped at home, would we have more time and energy to succeed in the workplace? We need wives!"

Flashbacks to my early working environment remind me of remarkable technological changes. After pounding manual typewriters for years, electric typewriters ZZZZ'd across the page when my fingers rested on keys. Dragged unwillingly into the computer age, I continued manual backup accounting methods until the computer's accuracy converted me into an enthusiastic disciple.

Glass ceilings hadn't been heard of in the 60s. Happy to have a job, unaware of goal-setting, not expecting promotions, women were oblivious of inequity issues. I was too naïve to realize I had cause for a lawsuit when the personnel supervisor advised my boss not to hire me because "her husband's family is too prolific."

The "wave of feminism" that started in the 1970s was less forceful than a trickle when it reached the rural Midwest in the mid-eighties. The male hierarchy reluctantly gave tiny raises to assertive women who, unafraid of conflict, faced off with bosses, but future advances were blocked for women branded with the "B" word.

EEO issues were ignored at our location. A visit from corporate officials gave me an invitation to dinner with the dignitaries. Trotting around in high heels, I pretended to belong in the male echelon with hopes my phony promotion would become real. Nope.

I'd expected to be judged by hard work, but a male mentor advised me I had to be political. "Phyllis, you just sit in your office and work. You have to get out and schmooze."

In the 1999 winter issue of Loyola, Micael Clarke, Ph.D. wrote, "My mother-in-law claims that my generation owes a great debt to her generation because they encouraged us to get as much education as we could . . . I hope that younger women will realize the opportunities they have today were not always there. My generation's gender revolution involved a lot of struggle . . . So you see, each generation owes a debt to the one before."

Yes! It took many years of perseverance for me to achieve any status within my working arena. Women younger than I moved up the ranks quickly, but some admitted: "You were a pioneer, Phyllis."

Younger women expect to achieve more. I warned my daughter not to set salary goals equal to her brother and brother-in-law. Fortunately, my daughter reached her goal despite my bad advice.

Have women's rights progressed with technology? Statistics say "No!" Facebook COO Sheryl Sandberg's new book, *Lean In,* restarted the conversation about working women's gender inequality in 2013. In her chapter, "Internalizing the Revolution," Sandberg wrote, "In 1970, American women were paid 59 cents for every dollar their male counterparts made. By 2010, women had protested, fought, and worked their butts off to raise that compensation to 77 cents for every dollar men made. As activist Marlo Thomas wryly joked on Equal Pay Day 2011, 'Forty years and eighteen cents. A dozen eggs have gone up ten times that amount.'"

There seems to be hope in the political arena. On September 28, 2013, ABCnews.go.com published the article, *Women Leaders Look Beyond the Glass Ceiling,* Emily's List President Stephanie Schrlock commented "There was no bathroom in the U.S. Senate for women in 1986 . . . . The good news is there was (recently) a traffic jam for the women's bathroom, so they're expanding the bathroom. But that took 28 years."

A magazine writer, Connie Schultz, after reading Sandberg's book, published an article in Parade on March 31, 2013: *A Million Ways to "Lean In".* with the subtitle *For working mothers, there's no such thing as one right path.* "Sandberg is right to encourage young women to imagine the biggest, brightest lives for themselves. I hope her book launches a million conversations."

The original title of my essay was *Four Decades Later*. Optimistically, ten years ago I wrote: "Supporting each other, we'll soar over our hurdles and smash through the glass ceilings!" Soaring? Only a few women have cracked the glass ceiling, and most of them endured a rite of passage with cuts and bruises to prove it.

Some women have pulled themselves up by the bootstraps. How much longer before women can soar? I'm hopeful that Sandberg's book will help more women sprout eagle wings.

The Shriver Report: A Woman's Nation Pushed Back from the Brink, released January 15, 2014, hopefully will empower women even more. The statistics are impressive and conclusive: Women have not been treated fairly. Sister Joan Chittister wrote in her essay included in the report: "Women are two-thirds of the poorest of the poor, because they lack access to the resources and recognition that men take for granted."

Maria Shriver predicts: "By pushing back and by putting into practice the solutions we're proposing in *The Shriver Report*, we can re-ignite the American Dream . . ."

Chapter 35
Sisters' Journeys
1997— 2013

      Four carloads arrive
      Until there are nine . . .
      Nine sisters divine.

      Nine sisters divine
      From Minnesota to Wisconsin drive . . .
      Drive to a retreat on Lake DesMoines.

      At a retreat on Lake DesMoines
      Irish silver tongues have begun . . .
      Begun endless conversation.

When the invitations arrive for the next Karsnia sisters' annual retreat, we open them immediately. We're all eager to see what awaits for us at the next get-together.

    Chattering reaches a crescendo after everyone has arrived and hugged. Like a hive of buzzing bees, we gather around the kitchen table, or out on the patio, or sip slushes in the sunshine down on the deck overlooking Lake DesMoines.

    There are traditions: Special themes and fine food, fun and laughter, brown bag gifts and gifts for pranks, continuing card tournaments and memory games.

    Colorful necklaces from New Orleans marked a Mardi Gras theme. High Tea with fresh-baked scones required picture hats and flowing scarves. Katherine, Peggy's friend from North Carolina, flew in to treat us to a spa weekend, serving as both maid and masseuse. A Style Show gave former 4-H queens an opportunity to model again.

    The Karsnia sisters consistently prove they are good cooks. Peggy's salads and desserts are tucked away in the refrigerators, Kay adds more. Susie's delicious caramel rolls entice everyone out of bed each morning, proving Susie's status as award-winning baker. Midge brings an unlimited supply of fresh fruit to serve at every meal in a watermelon bowl we all try to steal. Rosie helps her husband John catch fresh Walleye in Rainy Lake, which she fries to golden brown perfection.

One year, we drank coffee out of mugs inscribed with "Who Loves Ya, Baby?" provided by Peggy's Greek neighbor, Dino, whose gyros are popular at the state fair as well as at his restaurants. Drinking morning coffee from a mug proclaiming love is a great way to start the day!

Activities include walking and talking, swimming and sunning, snacking and eating, surprise gifts and competitive card tournaments are all part of the agenda. Hikers clog the road, moving from one group to another to join marathon conversations. Peggy's towel from her granddaughter summarizes changes: "I use to go skinny dippin', now I go chunky dunkin." Indeed, earlier years we did go skinny dipping in the moonlight, now our chunkier bodies refuse.

We love gifts! At any meal, little surprise gifts appear on plates: homemade jam or special soap or greeting cards—we love those thoughtful surprises. Mom started a special "birthday bash" tradition at the 1999 retreat, surprising us with gift-wrapped pricey panties. The first year Mom wasn't with us, Rosie took over the tradition; tears rolled down our cheeks as we opened our panties from "Mom."

Along with luggage, our secret brown bag gifts in grocery bags are smuggled in and placed on the fireplace hearth. Some bags hide treasures, some hide gags, some hide ugly recycled gifts, some hide sentimental gifts. Peggy's old Corelle dishes have "kept on giving" for years. Whether we get the good, bad or ugly—it's the luck of the dice!

Bags are opened with ear-splitting babble, new memories created. A favorite memory is of Eileen throwing a perfect candle ring of pansies across the room. "I just finished getting rid of junk, why would I want more!" The perennial pansies keep returning . . .

If you've heard a rumor that the Irish can talk—it's true! As the lone sister-in-law, it's my job to be the lone listener. Lying in bed listening to the babble of the early birds in the morning, I yell, "Does anybody have a listener?" Midge laughs, "Listening is not one of our talents." Early morning subdued conversations swell into a loud tidal wave when everyone is at the breakfast table. Peggy brews several pots of coffee to keep energy flowing. Mimosas, Susie's luscious caramel rolls, and Midge's fresh fruit bowls keep conversations lively.

Nothing stops those glib silver tongues. Thunder and lightning outside cannot compete with the voices reverberating inside. Heavy topics are discussed: religion and politics, diseases and medications, immorality and terrible TV shows, books and philosophy. Family issues are thoroughly covered: personal events, husbands, children and grandchildren.

There are always secrets and surprises. Sharp ears pick up an innocent comment and a clever surprise is created for the next year. Looking through photo albums one year, Rosie complained that she never ever had pretty shoes, wailing, "Look, here I am in my First Communion dress with ugly brown shoes!" Rosie's sorrow over brown shoes turned into a shower of shoes the following reunion, shoes of all sizes and colors: baby shoes, glamorous stilettos, worn out tennis shoes, and yes, more ugly brown shoes.

A raging wind kept wind chimes ringing and dinging one night, keeping me awake and grumpy. "Why would anyone hang wind chimes where people sleep?" Clanging wind chimes turned my complaining into chiming gifts the next year. Cheerfully, I hung them in trees all around my house—but none close enough to ruin my sleep!

One year, Aunt Harriet commented, "I never had a doll when I was growing up. We were too poor." At the next gathering, Aunt Harriet was surrounded by gifts. She unwrapped nine dolls. With tears in her eyes, she lovingly placed them in a hand-carved cradle made by her nephew, Tom Karsnia. Wiping her eyes, Aunt Harriet exclaimed, "At 84 years old I finally have dolls. I can't believe you did this for me!"

Mom was a forerunner in "Early Estate Planning." Wanting to be fair, she asked each daughter to choose one of her treasures, labeling it with the name. Susie was late to the party. "What would you like?" her mother asked. Susie picked out a decorative plate on the wall, but that was Peggy's. The second plate Rosie's; the third plate Kay's; the fourth plate Midge's. "No, Phyllis brought that plate back from Portugal for me—it's hers."

"Well, what can I have?" Susie wailed. Her mother pointed to a duck in the corner cabinet. "That's ugly! I don't want that ugly duck." At the next reunions, there were ducks for sixth place Susie! Ugly ducks, yellow rubber ducks, and a wooden duck Rosie had lovingly painted—getting her into hot water. Her daughter, Jean, reminded her: "That was my duck; I gave it to you to paint for me a long time ago."

One morning Kay sneaked up behind Eileen as she relaxed over morning coffee and placed. a diamond tiara on her head. "Eileen, you are crowned Queen for a Day!" With shocked delight Eileen shouted, "I remember that show. I always wanted to be queen." When Kay asked how many children she had, Eileen answered "Fifteen." Everyone gasped.

"Your washer and dryer must be worn out! We're giving you new ones." Eileen doubled over with laughter when Kay presented her with an old scrub board and a short clothesline with clothespins on it.

"What are your favorite things to read?" Kay asked. "Cookbooks," Eileen answered. Magically, nine presents were stacked at her chair—all cookbooks. Eileen read from *Treat Yourself: Recipes and Humor for Everyday*, "Too many cooks spoil the figure." Our reunions prove it!

One year, we all came bearing thank you gifts for Peggy, our annual hostess. Imagine Peggy's delight when she opened packages containing all the Corelle dishes she'd hidden in brown bags through the years. The ladies on *The View* had declared re-gifting a popular thing to do—and we gladly re-gifted the Corelles. Prolific Eileen gave an assortment of cups with a note: "Your cup mated with mine in my china cupboard, so now you have more!"

All the sisters have special talents and they were rewarded for them at a Polish Awards Ceremony. Kay, in a formal black suit and white shirt acted as Master of Ceremonies. She strutted in to announce, "Welcome to the Polish Awards Ceremony. My assistant is the lovely Rosalita." With balloons tucked in her black lace dress, Rosalita flitted in, tossing her long black wig as the sisters clapped and hooted. After the woo-woo's died down, Kay said, "There are talented celebrities competing for these awards!" Martha Stewart was a competitor in several categories, but the Karsnia clan crushed Martha with more losses than her stock debacle.

Stomachs aching from laughter, the sisters accepted clever awards: Eileen won the title of "Prolific-ness" for having fifteen children, beating out her mother and Old Woman in a shoe. Peggy, awarded a bucket of white paint, was named "Queen of White Paint" for the countless homes she painted white while moving from state to state. Susie received an egg beater, an ideal award for Best Baker. Chosen as Mae West look-a-like, Rosalita Rosie grinned and shook her fake boobs. Florence Nightingale didn't have a chance against Midge as Nurse of the Year. Aunt Harriet won as Quilter, Kay as Outstanding Teacher, and mine was Energetic Woman.

Pope John Paul and Queen Elizabeth lost "Longevity" to ninety-five-year-old Marie Karsnia. Her award was a basket containing some of her favorite things: A rosary to help her through the tough times, yarn and darning needle to keep her hands busy and productive, a deck of cards to play cribbage and whist, and a jar of pickles! A meal is not complete without pickles on the table.

The most memorable event was a Celebration of Life for Mom. After attending a friend's funeral, Mom wistfully said, "The church was full and her grandchildren gave beautiful eulogies." Rosie said, "Mom, you're going to have a bigger and better funeral." Mom retorted, "Then sit me up so I can watch!" Her daughters promptly planned a Celebration of Life. Friends, always eager to know what the sisters were planning for the next gathering, were stunned to hear, "We're having a funeral for our mother."

Kay came prepared with a script to narrate the Celebration of Life, some brought memorabilia for "show and tell." Not wanting it to be depressing, the "mourners" wore colorful gardening gloves and sunhats trimmed with flowers, solemnly filing into the sitting area—stifling giggles. As Master of Ceremonies, Kay announced: "Today, we are honoring a very special woman, Marie Donahue Karsnia, to share our memories and celebrate a life well lived! The young Marie wanted children, and children she got! Her eldest daughter, the one who also raised a big family, will share her thoughts."

Eileen: "You told us that you wanted us to sit you up at your funeral so you can enjoy it. Well, here you are." Tearfully, Eileen said, "I was very upset about moving to Alaska, begged Al not to go. Mom promised to write to me, but I didn't think she'd have time. She wrote to me nearly every day. If I got a letter I cried, and if I didn't get a letter I cried."

A voice from beyond said, "It only cost two cents to send it." *During the eulogies, we had to shush the deceased frequently, reminding her that the dead cannot talk. She paid no attention.*

Kay: Three boys later, (Leo, Tom, and Jack) Mom gave birth to Peggy. Peggy, what do you want to share?

Peggy: "I'm number six and I'm her favorite! I have wonderful memories of coming home from school and finding the kitchen filled with glazed donuts or caramel rolls. Mom set a good example of sharing with others. She gave us our faith in God and prayer. We love you and will miss you." Peggy's memorabilia honoring her mother was a Sunday Missal and white rosary beads.

Kay: "After Jim, along came Rosie.

Rosie: "I know that I'm the favorite because she tells me I am every time I come over. And when John and I had another baby late in life—Jaimie became the favorite grandchild. She's Mom's fiftieth. Rosie held up a dishtowel. "Peggy and I were giggling (as usual) and Mom put us outside. There we were, outside in the snow with only a little dishtowel to keep us warm—but we kept giggling. Mom, you've given us many memories and we'll always remember them and we'll always love you."

Kay: "Susie was born after Jerry. She's getting a Kitchen-Aid mixer now! Hooray!" *(All the sisters have Kitchen Aids except Susie. It's set in stone—she inherits her mother's).*

Susie: "Don't worry, Mom, I know I'm your favorite. You worked so hard: gardening, canning, washing clothes and cooking for a family of twelve. The best part is watching you at ninety-five. What a woman for a daughter to keep up to! I love you."

Kay; "After Mike and me, Baby Midge, who was premature and baptized at birth, came home from the hospital in a shoe box. She managed to survive."

Midge: "I was the last baby and Mom spoiled me. Mom, Dad and I had coffee and toast together every morning. It was our special time! Mom knew how much I hated housework and she let me go outside with Dad. Midge held up a jar with a hand-painted cover, saying, "Mom, I have a pacemaker in this jar so you can be at our parties for the rest of our lives. We love you, Mom."

Kay introduced Aunt Harriet. "It's not only daughters who are sharing their memories today. Dad's sister, Aunt Harriet met Marie as a young woman when she knocked Dad off his feet."

Aunt Harriet said: "Marie, my first memory of you was when you came to meet Rome's family in Frazee on your honeymoon. You stayed a few days and when you left I cried and cried because I didn't want you to go. Your honeymoon was nothing like honeymoons now. Romeo went off every day, helping family on their farms. My next memory was when you came to the Minnesota State Fair in the 1960s and stayed with us. If we wanted to find Rome, he was on Machinery Hill; if we wanted to find Marie, she was in the barn with the Jersey cows. I've looked forward to these reunions with your daughters. God has blessed me in many ways and He also blessed me with the love of a special sister-in-law."

Kay: "Her sons aren't here today to help us celebrate, but here's Leo's wife, Phyllis."

Phyllis: "I remember: Kids sitting shoulder-to-shoulder around a table bursting with huge platters of food. Chicken suppers every Sunday with chickens that first had to be killed and cleaned. Cleaning muddy vegetables fresh from the garden and peeling pounds of potatoes. Picking vegetables in the garden and canning them in August heat. The burns she suffered while taking the Thanksgiving turkey out of the oven, but never complaining about the pain she endured from the burns and the ulcers that followed throughout the years. She wonders why she's still here. I think it's because we all need her love."

Kay introduced herself: "I'm the eldest of the "little girls, Midge and me." *(Author note: Kay's eulogy gives the reader a glimpse into her mother's character and her life).* "My life is completely different than my mother's, but I love to bake and share it like she does. I remember helping with baking. Monday was wash day and I 'got to' fold the clothes from the line and sprinkle them. I didn't know I was helping with her work, I thought we were playing.

"Mom had health problems and had a serious accident with the Christmas turkey when I was about nine years old. But she took each medical milestone as it came; I guess she realized that there are things you can't change, so you ask for help from God and you go on.

"I wouldn't call Mom religious, but 'faith filled.' We prayed the rosary often and went to church, come hell or high water, every Sunday and Holy Day. Mom's involvement in the women's league meant volunteering *us* for help with church projects. In summing up my eulogy, I know Mom didn't plan to have twelve kids, but it surely was God's plan and she was a willing servant. Never did she say, 'I wish I didn't have so many kids.' Thanks, Mom! I learned a lot! I love you, and your Maker does too!"

Mom: "On his death bed, my dad told me, 'Rome always said he wanted a dozen children. If he does, you have them for him because you will be blessed.' And I have been blessed."

Throughout the Celebration of Life, Marie ignored our shushing. She made comments, laughed often, and shed happy tears. "Not everybody gets to have people tell them that they love them. I'm so lucky."

Kay continued: Mom has her tombstone ready: "Marie Karsnia lived from 1911 to— (dash)." She read *The Dash* by Linda Ellis. The "mourners" agreed that Marie is the perfect example of the dash: ". . . show appreciation more and love the people in our lives, and that . . . what mattered most of all was the dash between those years."

"Mom has a poem on her bathroom wall that says she'd rather receive one single rose when she was alive instead of dozens when she leaves this world. Mom, enjoy these flowers with our love." One by one, the "mourners" presented the living Marie with a long-stemmed pink rose, a hug, and a kiss. Eyes glowing, cheeks as pink as the ten fragrant roses on her lap, Marie joyfully posed with her family for her "funeral" photo.

After the emotional Celebration of Life, some took naps while others sipped slushes in the sunshine down on the deck. Love those slushes!

The sweet Karsnia women turn into demons during their whist tournaments. Mom and Kay partnered against Susie and Eileen. Onlookers crowded around the dining room table, watching. Nobody spoke as Mom dealt the cards. Susie said, "Just because you died doesn't mean I'm going to let you win the card game tonight." The tension thickened. "You dirty rat," Susie shouted more than once. Kay announced the scores of their winning hands loudly and frequently.

Marie's granddaughters invaded the party in the midst of shouting over the card game. The cousins, Sherry, Dawn, and Barb, had gathered at Jayne's cabin a couple miles away, anxious to join the fun their mothers bragged about each year. Greeting Grandma Marie with kisses, they expressed thankfulness that she was still alive after "The Wake." Marie repeated many times, "I'm so lucky to have so many love me."

> Voices and laughter resounding
> Crescendo surging
> Sisters bonding
> And reminiscing
> Stories and laughing
> Food and gifts generating
> Gratitude and joyfulness
> And LOVE.

At Marie Donahue Karsnia's real Celebration of Life after her death on January 26, 2008, the above sentiments were expressed again. At our next Sisters' gathering, we each brought our sympathy cards and albums honoring Marie. Reading the many kind words written about her was both emotional and healing.

The competitive card parties remained fierce; Midge took over Marie's chair to partner with Kay against Eileen and Susie. Escaping from the tension, Peggy, Rosie and Phyllis relaxed on the deck drinking in the beauty of red, gold, and green foliage. Screeching from the card game occasionally interrupted the September silence and solitude. Susie's words wafted over the lake: "Midge, you're channeling Mom. You hide in the weeds just like she did." We weren't surprised when Kay yelled out the door: "In case anyone's interested, Midge and I won!"

Marie's spirit remains with us.

* * *

Postscript: When Marie was eighty-six years old, she was chosen to participate as one of four elders to tell her history to school children. Larry Long, a traveling troubadour, recorded the stories of the four pioneers and worked with the school children to compose songs based on their lives.

Marie told the students: "I have a wonderful family and I think I'm a very lucky woman. I've had a lot of people to love, and a lot of people to love me." Marie's pride and love for her family inspired the theme of the song that the troubadour and the school children composed for her. At the Community Celebration held in October 1997 they energetically sang the song, *"To Have So Many Love Me."* In February, 2014, we found the International Falls, Minnesota Community Celebration posted on YouTube.

Chapter 36
Earthy Spirituality
Dove Island 1999-present

Bewildered by my new hobby, my friends asked, "Digging up rocks? Why?"

Why did I decide to turn a dense thicket into a rock garden? An article in a gardening magazine put me on this rocky path. Pictures of flowers and walking paths in a woodland garden inspired me to start clearing a dense thicket on our property. Logging off tall, scraggly trees searching for sunlight, I discovered a wall of rock with ferns flourishing on top, poking out of crevices. Uprooted trees exposed tips of rocks buried by decades of dirt, leaves, and pine needles. Shoveling and scraping, hoeing and hosing, gradually the rocks emerged.

Discovering beauty in the rocks filled me with joy. My home on Rainy Lake perches on historic rock carved by glaciers, part of a Canadian shield with some of the oldest exposed rocks in the world. I'm uncovering history! Native American Ojibwe paddling Rainy Lake lived on this land; our abstract lists the first owner as "Way-We-Quan-Aish-Kung, an Indian of the Boise Forte Tribe." French voyagers might have camped on these rocks. Furiously grubbing and hoeing, exposing Precambrian rock trod on by moccasins, I'm communing with spirits from centuries ago. Mysticism from the past permeates my present.

Baffled friends exclaimed, "Power washing rocks? Are you crazy?" On days that I wheedled my husband, Leo, to crank up the power washer, I sprayed for hours until the machine ran out of gas. My discoveries urged me on: rocks glittering with minerals or bejeweled with quartz, rocks with lacy patterns or unique formations from embedded roots. I looked at my rock creation and saw that it was good.

After revealing age-old glacial rocks, I started planting. Digging holes for plants provided another challenge; my shovel clinked against smaller rocks waiting to be rescued. Learning leverage techniques, I excavated rocks, surprising myself with my persistence. Occasionally, large rocks stubbornly clung to their hole, forcing me to call for my husband's muscles.

Vigorously hosing down the dirt, I often went slipping, sliding, and falling in the mud. Concerned about my safety, Leo built steps over the mud and a bridge over boulders on the edge of the lake.

Five months of hard labor resulted in a rock garden filled with hosta, ferns, and day lilies. From bags of river rock hauled from Menard's I created simulated river streams, adding a bench for a meditation spot. The bench beckons, but as I pass it I say, "I'm too busy to sit and meditate."

The rich humus from decades of composted leaves provided nourishment to lilac trees begging for more dirt on a rocky ridge. In the spring, sitting on a small deck Leo built in my "secret garden" on the rock, I inhale lilacs.

Nobody understood my passion for rocks, least of all me, until I went to St. Thomas Parish Mission *That They All May Be One*. The priests told us the mission was about changing us, to ask ourselves. "How do I see God? Where do I need to grow in my relationship with Creation? Where do I go to be moved by the Holy Spirit?"

A surprising number of people find beauty in nature, feeling closer to God out in the woods or on the lake or in their gardens. "Earth is sacred," the missionaries said. This was an "*aha* moment." Moved by the Holy Spirit to beautify the earth, uncovering rocks, digging them out of the dirt, I'd revealed hidden treasures. How many billions of years ago did the glaciers create this rock? How many millions of years ago did they drop these boulders? What history could this rock tell me? How many Ojibwe and French voyageurs trod on these rocks? I felt an affinity with nature and with native spirits.

Showing slides of the earth taken from the moon, the narrator said, "The earth is wondrous, fabulous, beautiful—and fragile. Humans are destroying our fragile earth."

It made me proud that I had worked tirelessly to beautify my little piece of the earth, uncovering fascinating rocks. I felt rich from working with the earth. I felt immense gratitude for living in such a spiritual place.

A FORMLESS WASTELAND

In a formless wasteland
Decades of dead leaves
Composted to host
Lilacs' perfume in the spring,
Hostas and ferns lively green,
Replace darkness with light.
I looked at my creation
And saw it was good.